Innovative Serging

Other books in the Creative Machine Arts series, available from Chilton:

Claire Shaeffer's Fabric Sewing Guide

The Complete Book of Machine Embroidery, by Robbie and Tony Fanning

Creative Nurseries Illustrated, by Debra Terry and Juli Plooster

Creative Serging Illustrated, by Pati Palmer, Gail Brown and Sue Green

The Expectant Mother's Wardrobe Planner, by Rebecca Dumlao

The Fabric Lover's Scrapbook, by Margaret Dittman

Friendship Quilts by Hand and Machine, by Carolyn Vosburg Hall

Know Your Bernina, by Jackie Dodson

Know Your Elna, by Jackie Dodson with Carol Ahles

Know Your New Home, by Jackie Dodson with Judi Cull and Vicki Lynn Hastings

Know Your Pfaff, by Jackie Dodson with Audrey Griese

Know Your Sewing Machine, by Jackie Dodson

Know Your Singer, by Jackie Dodson

Know Your Viking, by Jackie Dodson with Jan Saunders

Sew, Serge, Press, by Jan Saunders

Sewing and Collecting Vintage Fashions, by Eileen MacIntosh

Other books by the authors, available from Chilton:

Creative Serging Illustrated

Distinctive Serger Gifts and Crafts, An Idea Book for All Occasions

Innovative Sewing, The Newest, Best, and Fastest Techniques

Ordering Information:

For ordering information, see page 174.

Special Offer:

For a free sampler of articles and ideas from past issues of *Serger Update*, send a business-sized, self-addressed, stamped envelope to: *Serger Update* Sampler Offer, 2269 Chestnut, Suite 269BK, San Francisco, CA 94123.

Innovative Serging

The Newest, Best, and Fastest
Techniques for Overlock Sewing

Gail Brown and Tammy Young

Chilton Book Company
Radnor, Pennsylvania

Published in Radnor, Pennsylvania 19089, by Chilton Book Company

Color photographs by Lee Phillips
Designed by Martha Vercoutere
Illustrations by Chris Hansen
Samples sewn by Naomi Baker and Virginia Fulcher

Manufactured in the United States of America

Library of Congress Cataloging in Publication Data

Brown, Gail.
    Innovative serging: the newest, best, and fastest techniques for overlock sewing/Gail Brown and Tammy Young.

    p. cm.—(Creative machine arts series)
    Bibliography: p. 174
    Includes index.
    1. Serging. I. Young, Tammy.
II. Title. III. Series.   89-42854
TT713.B75 1989   CIP
646.2'044—dc20
ISBN 0-8019-7986-2

3 4 5 6 7 8 9 0   8 7 6 5 4 3 2 1 0

Contents

Foreword by Nancy Zieman..............vii
Preface: The Story Behind
    Innovative Serging.....................viii
Acknowledgments.............................. ix
Introduction.......................................x
1. **Serged Fashion Features**.................1
    Fast-Serged Fashion
        Details
    Wrapped Collar Blouse
    Breakthrough: Serged
        Zipper Applications
    Edge-Finishing Update
    Serged-Chain Gathering
    Contoured Covers for
        Shoulder Pads
2. **Borrowing the Best From
    Ready-to-Wear**.............................14
    Copying the Industrial
        Cover Stitch
    Faux Flatlocking
    Johnny Collars: An Easy
        Crew Combo
    Modular Knit Know-How
    Serge-Finished Ribbing
    Sleek Wraps: A Seventh
        Avenue Trend
    Snazzy Serged Reversibles
    Criss-crossed Belt Loops
    Ready-to-Wear Elastic
        Applications
    Exposed Elastic Bands
    The Two-Step Topstitched
        Casing
    Elasticized Binding
    Elastic Shirring

3. **Yes, You Can Serge
    Jackets and Coats**.........................32
    Speediest Serged Tailoring
    Soft Tailoring: Savvy
        Serging Strategies
    Serging Boiled Wool
        (Beautifully)
4. **The Newest Decorative
    Threads, Techniques,
    and Stitches**.................................40
    The Latest on Threads
    The Latest Decorative
        Techniques
    Decorative Serging: Ten
        Steps to Success
    How Will Decorative
        Serging Look on Your
        Garment?
    The Latest Stitches: 3/4-
        Thread Innovations
    Flatter Flatlocking
5. **Serged Embellishments** 51
    Invisible (Well, Almost)
        Embellishment
        Secrets
    Serged Piping
    Serged Scrollwork:
        Couching
    Fishing Line Flounces
    Serging Bead Strands
    Serged Appliqués
    Serger Cutwork?
6. **Update: The Latest on
    Serging Sweaters**.........................68
    Secrets for Serging
        Cotton and Other
        Stretchy
        Sweaterknits
    Speedy Knit-and-Serged
        Sweaters

7. Dressed-up Serging............................76
   Basic Strategies
   Custom Finishes
   Serged Glitz
8. Fast-Serged Accessories.................. 83
   Twist-to-Fit Sash
   Serged Ribbing Rose
   Pocket Squares
   Quick Knit
     Accessories
   Quick Serged Cover-up
**9. Maximum Efficiency, Minimal
   Time: Production-Order
   Serging**..94
   Planning Considerations
     and Questions
   Implementing Basic Plans
10. Alter, Fit, and Restyle..................102
   Rapid Unraveling of
     Serged Stitches
   Fine-Tuning Fit
   Instant Alterations
   Better Sweaters for Less:
     Serged Fitting &
     Restyling
   Serge Menswear into
     Women's Wear
11. Fabric Decorating—in a Flash.....112
   Napkin Know-How,
     Updated
   Serged Napkin Rings
   Never-Miss Mitered
     Placemats
   Serged Sheet Covers
   Serger-Strip Patchwork
     and Quilting
   Instant Draped Curtains
   Circle Curtains
   Quick Cord Cover-ups
   Serged Decorations: Replace
     Paper With Fabric

**12. Making the Most
   of Your Serger**............................134
   Simple Steps to
     Improving Stitch
     Quality
   Serger Troubleshooting
     with Sue Green
   Neat Feet
   Hot Serger Hints
   Serger Smarts: Tips from
     the Sergeon
**13. Machine Update: A Guide
   to Smart Serger Shopping**.........146
   Features: Key Questions
     and Considerations
   Considering a Five-
     Thread Serger?
   Serger Cutting
     Attachments
   Buying the Right Serger
     Needle
   Serger Needle Guide
Glossary of Stitches.............................157
Sources...162
   Serger Companies
   Serge-by-Mail Directory
References..174
   Serger Books
   Update Newsletter Serger
     Booklets
   Serger Videos
   Sewing Publications
About the Authors..............................178
Index...179

Foreword

By Nancy Zieman

Seven years ago when I pulled my "mail-order serger" out of the box, I stared at it in the same wonder as looking under my car's hood! After a 45-minute threading ordeal, I managed to serge an overlock stitch and thought, "Why did I order this?" Thankfully, Gail and Tammy did not have any such doubts.

Instead, Gail was testing, researching, and most importantly writing to bring us some of the first detailed serging information. Her pursuit didn't stop with her first co-authored book, *Sewing With Sergers*. With the advent of each new serger thread/ ribbon, notion, and machine development, she persevered, bringing us the most up-to-the-minute information that went beyond the basics to the creative. Be assured that Gail will continue to experiment. She shares her latest findings in *Innovative Serging*.

Her collaborator, Tammy Young, is known for her *Update Newsletters* in serging and sewing. She is a master at presenting innovative techniques in a concise, easy-to-understand format with graphics and illustrations that have fashion flair. Tammy is enthusiastic about the advantages and potential that sergers have allowed home sewers. *Innovative Serging* details the techniques that will make your serger work for you.

Together, Gail and Tammy have pooled their talents in the writing of *Innovative Serging*. This book details the most up-to-date techniques for serging all sorts of items—casual clothing, sportswear, home decorating, holiday wear, etc. You'll soon find yourself busily serging and wondering why you had waited so long.

Gail and Tammy have taken the mystery out of serging. You'll use this book many times, so keep it handy. Now, about my car. . . .

Preface

The Story Behind
Innovative Serging

Sergers have captivated home sewers everywhere, with sales of overlock machines and related products booming. While a serger was originally considered as a machine for seam finishing only, ingenious enthusiasts are always expanding the bounds of this small workhorse's creative limits.

Several home-sewing publications were and are devoting space to serger sewing, but none has focused on the subject in-depth and exclusively. In response to the growing need for an all-serger information source, Tammy introduced *Serger Update* in April, 1987; as in her successful *Sewing Update* newsletter, the emphasis of *Serger Update* was on the latest techniques. Gail collaborated as Contributing Editor and featured columnist.

Sewing Update and *Serger Update* hire professional industry writers who not only analyze but also originate some of the newest information, trends, and techniques. Cooperative efforts multiply the creativity; ideas from one writer are often tested and expanded by another, all in the interest of achieving top quality construction, serged or sewn in the shortest time possible. Because the newsletters don't accept advertising, they are uniquely positioned to present objective information that is selected in consideration of reader survey responses.

When Robbie Fanning suggested that our research be integrated into two books, *Innovative Serging* and *Innovative Sewing,* we welcomed the opportunity.

Our intent for *Innovative Serging* was to assemble and organize all the ingenious and timesaving methods developed after the release of *Creative Serging Illustrated* (see page 174), which Gail coauthored. The criterion for included material was demanding: unprecedented or significantly improved serger techniques not found in any other book. And because we don't believe in serging when sewing is the better alternative, you'll notice that many of our projects incorporate tandem technology, combining overlock and conventional machine stitching.

The time we spent experimenting and making mistakes will save you time; for each application, we tried several approaches before arriving at our favorite, that is, the most practical method that produced the best results. *Our goal was to produce results for you, so that after reading only a few pages you'd be able to quickly master a serger technique never before tried or used successfully up to this point.* And it is our hope that whenever you refer to this book, it will provide the confidence and know-how you need to overcome any serging challenge.

Gail Brown and Tammy Young

Acknowledgments

Our special thanks to the knowledgeable sewing professionals who have written for our *Serger Update* newsletters, helping us develop the materials included in this book: Naomi Baker, Ann Beyer, Karen Dillon, Karen Kinney Drellich, Sue Green, Gale Grigg Hazen, Hazel Boyd Hooey, Janet Klaer, Nancy Kores, Ann Price, Jan Saunders, Barbara Weiland, Leslie Wood and Nancy Zieman.

Also, this book could not have been written without the ongoing support of and essential information from the major serger companies and their local dealers. Our thanks to the following firms (listed in alphabetical order and paired with their respective brand names): Bernina of America (Bernette and FunLock); Brother International Corp. (Homelock); Elna, Inc. (Elnalock and Elnita); Fabri-Centers of America (Toyota); Juki Industries of America (Juki Lock); New Home Sewing Machine Co. (MyLock and Combi); Pfaff American Sales (HobbyLock); Riccar America (Riccar Lock); Simplicity Sewing Machines (Easy Lock); Singer Sewing Machine Co. (Ultralock); Tacony Corp. (Baby Lock and Serge-Mate); Viking Sewing Machine Co. (Huskylock); and White Sewing Machine Co. (Superlock). Addresses are listed on page 162.

It's also been a considerable advantage to work with Naomi Baker, a writer (coauthor of *Distinctive Serger Gifts and Crafts*) and arguably the finest serger seamstress anywhere. She will, we are certain, serge with, over, or on anything. Her input was invaluable, whether it was in initiating methods, determining technique feasibility, or editing steps to guarantee your serging success.

In addition, we applaud Chris Hansen, who single-handedly produced the illustrations for this book. As our newsletter artist, fellow sewing enthusiast, and friend, he continues to provide inspiration, encouragement, and enlightened critique of our techniques.

Finally, we thank our editor, Robbie Fanning, a real pro who always encourages the possibilities.

Easy-Knit®, Decor-Bond®, Pellon®, Quilter's Fleece®, ShirTailor®, Style-A-Shade® and *Wonder-Under™* are all registered trademarks of The Pellon Company, a division of Freudenberg Nonwovens Limited Partnership. *Easy-Knit®* and *Style-A-Shade®* were formerly sold by Stacy Industries; when Stacy Industries went out of business, these products were purchased by Pellon.

Introduction

How to Make This Book Work for You

We know you never have enough reading or sewing time, so we tried to organize our information to make the most of the moments you have to spare. In brief:

• **Read as little or as much as you like.** This book is organized modularly, so one project or chapter is not dependent on another. If there are cross-references, page numbers are cited. As a guideline, Chapters 1 through 10 are fashion techniques and projects, Chapter 11 covers fabric decorating, and the rest of the book is a compilation of handy reference and hard-to-find source information.

• **Find specific techniques within the chapters** by referring to the Index, on pages 179-181.

• **Look up unfamiliar stitches and terms in the Glossary,** pages 157-161 and the Index.

• **Skim the book quickly for focusing on the fashion or project illustrations** that immediately follow chapter sub-head introductions.

• **Regard any reference to straight stitching as straight stitching on a conventional sewing machine.** Except where needed for clarity, we do not specify conventional straight stitching.

• **Regard any reference to serging as 3-thread overlocking,** unless otherwise specified. For other serge-seaming, serge-finishing, and decorative stitch options, see the "Glossary of Stitches," pages 157-161.

• **Note sources for products listed** at the end of related techniques and projects. Addresses are given on pages 163-173 in the "Serge-by-Mail Directory."

• **Consult** *Creative Serging Illustrated* (see page 174) **or the other books and videotapes** described in "References," pages 174-177, for basic serging information.

1. *Serged Fashion Features*

Many of you have asked us, *"Are there ways I can use my serger to speed sewing of collars, facings, cuffs, or even zippers?"* In fact, a surprising number of what we call fashion features can be serged. Serging not only speeds seaming and finishing but also eliminates time-consuming clipping and enhances durability by ravel-proofing edges.

Fast-Serged Fashion Details

You're sold on the virtues of serging knits and sportswear. Now put your serger to work improving the look and quality of detailing on dresses and blouses made of *any woven or knit fabric*.

• Don't hesitate to serge **delicate fabrics** like silk broadcloth, polyester crepe, or rayon challis. Finishing soft, ravel-prone fabrics with conventional zigzagging can be slow and marginally effective, plus it can cause bulky tunneling. With fast-serged finishing, however, the same seams can lie smooth, flat, and ravel-free for the life of the garment. Try 3/4-thread finishing on especially ravelly fabrics. See Fig. 1-1. Change to

Fig. 1-1

a smaller and/or new serger needle for these lighter, softer fabrics. Remember, your thread size should be proportionate to the smaller needle size; try special serger- or lingerie-weight thread.

• Decide whether to serge the **seams** of your garment or to just serge-finish the raw edges. (Serged seams should be used only on semi-fitted or loosely fitted styles that won't threaten to strain the narrow allowances.) Opt for serge-finishing heavier and loosely constructed knits or wovens. Test first. Sergers, like conventional machines, are adjusted for sewing more than one layer of fabric, so loops may hang off the edge when finishing a single layer. If so, tighten the looper tensions. It's easiest to finish the edges before seaming; skim off only edge hairs for accurate gauging of the allowance width when seaming later. Start by serge-finishing all the vertical seam edges, then move to the horizontal.

• **In-seam pockets** can present serging problems. For easier handling, serge-finish the pocket pieces before straight-stitching them to the garment, starting at the tops and trimming off any sharp corners (rather than stopping to turn corners). The fit at the side seam won't be altered. See Fig. 1-2.

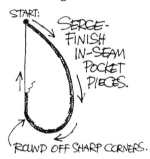

Fig. 1-2

• Create **tunnel tucks**, like those shown on the dress on page 1, with flatlocked topstitching. Don't allow the upper looper stitches to hang over the edge. Then, tighten the needle tension incrementally to achieve a slightly raised or tunneled tuck stitch. Because this tuck doesn't take up much or any fabric (depending on the flatlock width), it can be added after the garment has been cut out. Flatlock with a narrow rolled-edge stitch for a mock

pin tuck. Or, flatlock over a 1/8" ribbon to accent the tuck. See Fig. 1-3.

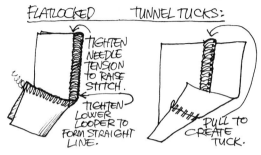

Fig. 1-3

• Contradictory to what you've probably been told or taught, serging is great for seaming **round collars**, and in just one step. There's no need for trimming or clipping as is done in the conventionally stitched method; the serging is narrow enough to be bulk-free and to turn smoothly. From the right side, understitch the serged seam to the undercollar with straight-stitching. Lace or sheer collars are wonderful made in the same manner; for lace, use organza for the undercollar and, if possible, narrow the stitch (understitching is unnecessary). The seam that shows through is always even and uniformly finished. See Fig. 1-4.

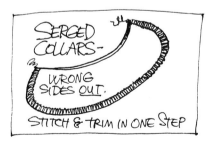

Fig. 1-4

• The same principle applies to **facing applications.** Interface, then finish the facing edge with serging (a welcome relief from bulky, time-consuming clean finishing). Place the facing right sides together on the edge and serge the seam. Again, the result is a flat, smooth, more durable seam that requires no trimming or clipping. From the right side, understitch the serged seam to the facing with straight-stitching. See Fig. 1-5.

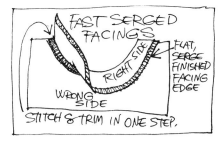

Fig. 1-5

☞ **Update tip:** Press serge-seamed collars and facings carefully, if at all, to prevent a conspicuous seam impression on the right side. Note that understitching generally facilitates smooth turning and minimizes the need for pressing.

• **Sleeve cuffs** can also be serge-seamed. If the corners are rounded, seam as described for the rounded collar. If the corners are squared, serge the long edge, right sides together. Then wrap the long edge allowance *toward* the undercuff and serge the short ends: to prevent jamming when

seaming, serge from the raw edges *toward* the seamed edge (Fig. 1-6).

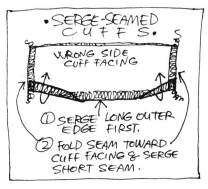

Fig. 1-6

Secure seam ends with seam sealant, allow to dry, and trim tails. Turn the cuff right sides out. (Other applications for wrapped seams are explained in the next section, "Wrapped Collar Blouse," pages 4-7.)

• For a **seamed placket,** apply the cuff with serging, as shown (Fig. 1-7).

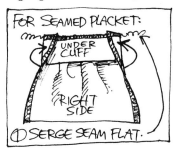

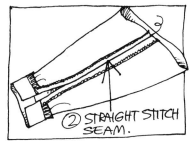

Fig. 1-7

(Step-by-step instructions for converting from a standard to a seamed placket are given in Nancy Zieman's *The Busy Woman's Sewing Book*, available through Nancy's Notions. See "Sources," page 174).

• To minimize bulk at **waistline seams**, straight-stitch and then serge-finish the edges together. If the seam also doubles as an elastic casing, add 1" seam allowances; stitch the seam, finish the edges with serging, stitch the casing, and feed the elastic through.

• Light, breezy **hems** can be quickly and professionally machine-stitched. After properly hanging and marking from the floor, trim the hem to 3/4". Finish with serging, trimming off 1/4". To ease the edge of flared hems, use your serger's differential feed at the 1:2 ratio setting or "ease plus" with forced hand-feeding. Turn up the hem and lightly press. Using the presser foot as a stitching width guide, topstitch the hem in place from the right side. See Fig. 1-8.

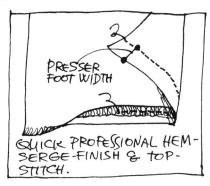

Fig. 1-8

Wrapped Collar Blouse

Want to sew a blouse in the quickest possible time without sacrificing construction quality? Try combining the speed of serger sewing with the durable straight-stitch of a conventional machine. Using the new wrapped corner technique, you can do what was once considered impossible—**serge corner seams.**

Materials Needed:
• **Blouse pattern.** It should have a shallow sleeve cap requiring minimum easing.

• **Blouse fabric.** Use tightly constructed fabric if serging a blouse with decorative exposed edges. For a reversible look, use contrasting color facings and pocket lining.

• **Fusible interfacing.** Try Easy-Knit, Fusible for Feather to Midweight Fabrics, Sheer Blenders by Pellon, or any similar product. (Test first on scraps of blouse fabric.)

• **Seam sealant.** Try Fray Check™ or No-Fray™ or any similar product.

- **Decorative serger thread.** This is needed for the exposed seam style (loopers only). Try buttonhole twist, lightweight rayon (30- or the lighter 40-weight), woolly stretch nylon, or pearl cotton (size 5 or the finer size 8). Or, use two strands of all-purpose thread in each looper.

Preparation of Machines, Pattern Pieces, and Fabrics

- *Place your serger adjacent to your conventional machine for easy access* to the dual construction techniques described here. Set up the serger for standard 3-thread seaming, and the conventional machine for 10 to 12 stitches per inch straight-stitching.

- For interfacing patterns, trim 1/2" from the seams on the collars, cuffs, and facing patterns.

- To create the proper roll, trim 1/4" from the long outer edge of the undercollar.

- Because seam allowances will be trimmed by the serger, mark notches, dots, and other pattern markings on the seamline. Use water-erasable pen or tailor's chalk.

Sequence for Serge-seaming and Serge-finishing

1. Right sides together, serge the collar to the undercollar along the long outer edge, as shown in Fig. 1-9.

Fig. 1-9

2. Press the seam allowance flat and then down, toward the undercollar. This forms the wrapped seam. See Fig. 1-10.

Fig. 1-10

☞ **Update tip:** After pressing, understitch with straight-stitching, through all the seam layers (1/8" from the seamline on the undercollar side). This stitching will keep the seamline defined and flat.

3. Serge the collar ends right sides together, as shown above (Fig. 1-10). *(The seam serged in Step 1 should still be wrapped down toward the undercollar.)* Press the seams flat. Turn the collar right sides out and press again.

4. Serge the shoulder seams.

5. Pin the collar to the neckline, matching dot and center back markings.

6. Serge-finish the outer edges of the front facing pieces. Pin the front facing to the neckline, sandwiching the collar between, as shown (Fig. 1-10). If working with a one-piece front and facing, simply fold along the indicated fold line right sides together and skip Step 8, below.

7. Serge the neckline seam. (Remove pins when they reach the front of the foot.) Press the seam flat. Press again, *wrapping the seam allowance down toward the facing, as shown.* See Fig. 1-11.

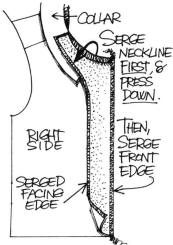

Fig. 1-11

8. Serge the front facing seams right sides together, holding the wrapped seam toward the blouse facing (Fig. 1-11). Turn the facings right sides out and press to align the seamline along the edge.

9. Finish the sleeve hem edges with serging; turn up and topstitch with straight-stitching.

10. Pin the sleeves into the armholes, matching markings. Serge the seams.

11. Pin the sleeve/underarm seams right sides together. *Make sure the sleeve hem edges match.* Starting at the sleeve hem edges, serge the seam through to the bottom hem edges.

12. Finish the bottom hem edge with serging; turn up and topstitch with a conventional straight-stitch.

13. Complete the remaining blouse details according to the pattern instructions.

Sequence for Decorative Serging

Once you've mastered the quick-serged blouse basics, graduate to decorative serging. *Keep in mind that the serging order is different,* as outlined below.

Prepare your serger by threading the upper and lower loopers with the decorative thread(s) of your choice. (Good all-around choices are woolly stretch nylon, 30- or 40-weight rayon, or machine embroidery threads.) Adjust for narrow balanced or rolled, short satin serging, fine-tuning the width and length on similar-grain blouse scraps. The thread on your conventional machine should match or blend with the decorative thread used on the serger.

1. Interface the collar and facing pieces. Before fusing in place, trim the interfacing 3/4" along all the seam edges. The trimming will prevent the interfacing from showing along the decoratively serged edges.

2. Pin the front facings to the blouse, wrong sides together. Decoratively serge the front edges (*not the neckline*).

3. Serge the shoulder seams, wrong sides together. Press the seam to the back of the blouse and edge-stitch in place with straight-stitching.

4. Serge the outer edge and ends of the collar, wrong sides together. If using lighter weight decorative thread, simply chain off the corners and apply seam sealant; trim the chain tails after

the sealant has dried. For neater finishing when using heavier decorative thread, turn the corners or chain off and weave the thread chain tail under the serging.

5. Pin the upper collar to the wrong side at the neckline, matching markings. Serge to the neckline as shown (Fig. 1-12). To secure threads at the corner, refer to Step 4.

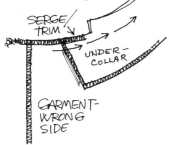

Fig. 1-12

☞ **Update tip:** After serging the collar to the blouse, reinforce at the collar notch (Fig. 1-13) with straight-stitching.

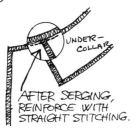

Fig. 1-13

6. Finish the blouse following Steps 9 to 13 on page 60. *Optional:* Hem the sleeve, bodice, and pocket with decorative flatlocking.

✎ **Note:** For more details on and applications for Nancy Zieman's innovative wrapped collar technique, refer to *The Busy Woman's Sewing Book,* from Nancy's Notions (see page 174).

Breakthrough: Serged Zipper Applications

"Don't serge zippers." That's what overlock experts have been telling us for years. But serging zippers is a surprisingly fast and durable alternative to conventional lapped applications. The zipper is inserted and the fabric edges are finished simultaneously. Necessarily exposed, this serged zipper method minimizes bulk in covers of all kinds and provides fast, decorative openings in casual tops or totes.

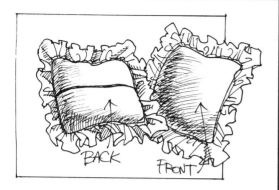

All you need is a zipper and a place to put it. Although lightweight nylon coil zippers feed particularly smoothly under the serger foot, we've also had good luck serging heavier upholstery zippers. A piping foot (see page 140) is also helpful, because the channel on the underside of the foot accommodates the zipper teeth. This foot isn't available for all brands or every model serger, but some feet are interchangeable among brands. Check with your local dealer. Luckily, our testing has proved that while **a piping foot ensures smooth stitching, it isn't essential.**

1. Use a zipper at least 4" longer than the opening. Unzip the zipper so that the pull is at the bottom. Place the zipper tape face down on the right side of the fabric (allow 5/8" seams), centering the zipper teeth over the seamline. *The zipper tape should extend 2" beyond the opening at both ends* so you can then

serge without catching the foot on the metal pull or stops. See Fig. 1-14.

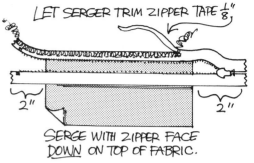

Fig. 1-14

2. With the wrong side of the zipper on top, serge the tape, *trimming it and the fabric about 1/8"* (or any excess width—the heavier the zipper, the wider the tape). See Fig. 1-14. (Stitch with either a balanced 3- or 3/4-thread overlock stitch, about 5-6 mm. wide.) From the right side, press all layers away from the coil; use a press cloth to protect heat-sensitive nylon zippers.

3. Zip the zipper. Right sides together, align the other fabric edge with the other side of the zipper. Pin to the tape. Unzip the zipper. Serge the fabric to the tape, trimming both layers about 1/8" (see Fig. 1-15). From the right side, press all layers away from the coil.

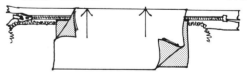

Fig. 1-15

4. Zip the zipper. To prevent the pull from coming off the coil track, bartack as shown with a conventional machine and matching thread. (To bartack, adjust for a wide zigzag stitch, at "0" length, or with the feed dogs dropped.) See Fig. 1-16.

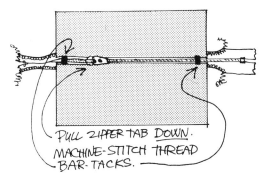

PULL ZIPPER TAB DOWN.
MACHINE-STITCH THREAD BAR-TACKS.

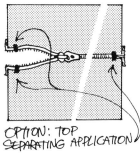

OPTION: TOP SEPARATING APPLICATION

Fig. 1-16

5. Finish the project by serge-seaming over the zipper tape at both ends. (Note the difference between a nonseparating and separating application.) For a nonseparating application, the tape ends can be stitched in the facing

seam. Whether or not the bartacks show is personal preference. See Fig. 1-17.

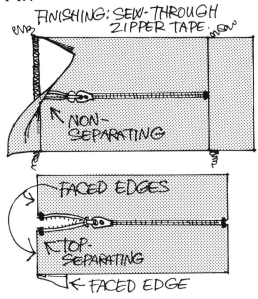

FINISHING: SEW-THROUGH ZIPPER TAPE. sew

NON-SEPARATING

FACED EDGES

TOP-SEPARATING

FACED EDGE

Fig. 1-17

☞ **Update tip:** If the zipper pull comes off the coil, remove the metal stop and from the bottom, slide the pull back on the coil.

Sources: For zippers of every weight, color, and type imaginable, try The Bee Lee Company, Custom Zips, Jacquart's, The Rain Shed, and Solo Slide Fasteners. (For addresses, see "Serge-by-Mail Directory," pages 166-168).

Edge-Finishing Update

How can you take sewing shortcuts without shortchanging quality? Undoubtedly you count on fast-serged edge-finishing to be one of your most

SERGING FINISHES TOP & SHORTS EDGES.

reliable timesavers. But if you've been disappointed in the durability of serge-finished edges, here are some technique improvements to try:

• When finishing decoratively (seams out), **face the edge first, wrong sides together.** (To enhance the stability and body of the facing, interface the facing with a lightweight fusible interfacing.) This is a philosophy change from the early days of single-edge decorative finishing. (**Gail's note:** I learned the hard way—most of my samples didn't

withstand a season of classes.) The majority of fabrics, whether knit or woven, simply don't have the body, weight, or tight construction that single-edge finish demands. (Consider that a conventionally faced edge is reinforced with straight-stitching, understitching, and at least four layers of fabric.) Use the facing provided in your pattern, narrowing or widening it as you like. When using ravelly fabrics, start by serge-finishing the facing edge. See Fig. 1-18. Or, use a 1"-wide strip of bias self-fabric as a facing.

STABILIZE WITH FACING—SERGE WRONG SIDES TOGETHER.

Fig. 1-18

☞ **Update tip:** If using a loosely constructed, heavier fabric, face with a more stable but lighter weight fabric. For example, use single-knit jersey to face velour, broadcloth for corduroy, and doubleknit for sweaterknit.

• **Stabilize turn-and-stitch finishing with transparent (polyurethane) elastic.** Adding this elastic element discourages stretching and stitch popping along bias edges and edges subjected to lots of wear, like necklines. (It's great for wrapped styles.) Pretrim the edge allowance to 3/8" (for 1/4"-wide elastic) or 1/2" (for 3/8"-wide elastic). Place the elastic on the wrong side of the edge in a 1:1 ratio. From the wrong side, serge the edge, through the elastic, trimming the fabric edge if necessary. Turn to the wrong side and topstitch with a single or double needle. For more stability, stretch the elastic slightly when applying. See Fig. 1-19.

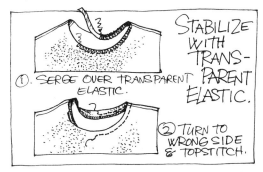

Fig. 1-19

• **Stabilize with piping.** Create your own serger piping (see "Simple Serged Piping," pages 52-56) or use the purchased variety. With a zipper foot on your conventional machine, straight-stitch the piping to the edge right sides together. Stitch directly over the piping stitching line. Turn the piping allowances to the wrong side and edge-stitch from the right side to secure. See Fig. 1-20. *Optional:* Serge-finish the piping raw edges before edge-stitching.

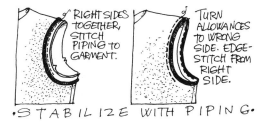

Fig. 1-20

Variation: Piping can be serge-seamed to the edge, although around tight curves this method is trickier than straight-stitching. A piping foot (see page 140) will help prevent skewing off the piping as you serge, but it isn't mandatory. For even piping, the needleline of the serged seam should stitch directly over the piping stitching line; adjust the serged stitch width and trim accordingly.

Sources: For transparent elastic—Clotilde, Nancy's Notions, Serge and Sew Notions, and Stretch & Sew Fabrics. (See "Serge-by-Mail Directory," pages 166-168, for addresses.)

Serged-Chain Gathering

Yes, you can gather serging, even when it's stitched on denim or heavy canvas. This ingenious method, developed by John Harris of Juki Industries of America, differs from most methods currently taught or published in that the serger thread strands are used to pull up the gathering, rather than a separate heavy thread.

✎ **Note:** Use either a 3-thread or 3/4-thread, wide, balanced stitch for this technique. However, if using a 3/4-thread serger without a slotted foot, it's easier if you convert to 3-thread stitching.

1. First, **set the needle tension(s) to "0" and raise the presser foot.** This will allow you to easily pull on the chain (to the left); simultaneously, turn the handwheel back and forth with quick, short turns in a rocking manner.

Instead of a chain, there will now be four (or three) separate threads, as shown. See Fig. 1-21. *Pull out a little*

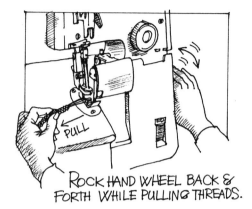

ROCK HAND WHEEL BACK & FORTH WHILE PULLING THREADS.

Fig. 1-21

more thread than the length of the edge to be gathered.

2. Return needle tensions to balanced stitch settings. Adjust for a medium-length and full-width stitch.

3. Place the fabric edge to be gathered under the foot. *Serge just one stitch on the fabric* and raise the needle(s).

4. Position the unchained threads just pulled out under the foot, as shown in Fig. 1-22. On some machines, there's a

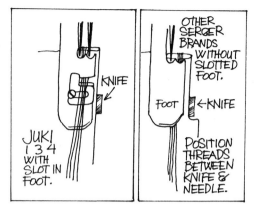

Fig. 1-22

slot in the foot with a movable finger guide (Fig. 1-23); position the movable

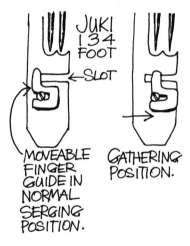

Fig. 1-23

finger guide more to the right so the threads can be guided between the two needles without sewing over them.

5. Bring the threads through the slot, twisting slightly to form one strong cord. *No slot in your presser foot?* Sim-

ply bring the threads over the front of the foot (butted up against the right foot ledge) between the needle and the knife. See Fig 1-23.

6. Now serge, *keeping the thread cord between the needle and the knife* (serge over the cord, but not through it). See Fig. 1-24. At the end of the fabric,

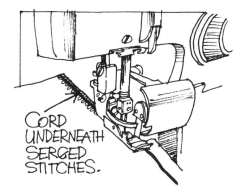

Fig. 1-24

move the cord to the left of the knife to prevent cutting. Gather even the heaviest fabric by simply pulling on the thread cord (Fig. 1-25).

Fig. 1-25

Contoured Covers for Shoulder Pads

Our talented illustrator, Chris Hansen, is a sewing and serging enthusiast. With his annotated drawings, Chris showed us his preferred method for covering contoured shoulder pads.

✎ **Note:** If covered flat, pads tend to remain flat, protruding out rather than lying flush with the shoulders. Because this pad is covered in the curved position with the top down on the machine plate, the fit-to-the-shoulder shape is retained. See Fig. 1-26.

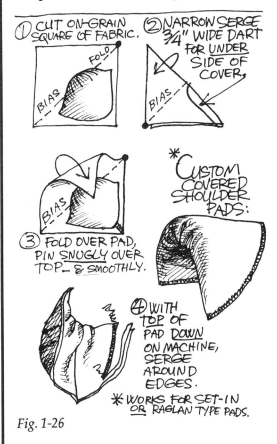

Fig. 1-26

2. Borrowing the Best From Ready-to-Wear

Ready-to-wear provides us with unequaled inspiration for serging applications. After all, manufacturers have been serging for over 60 years; fragile profit margins demand shortcut sewing methods that won't short-change the finicky fashion customer. Borrow the best of manufacturing methods to maximize your time and the use of your serger while multiplying your fashion possibilities.

Copying the Industrial Cover Stitch

In our pursuit of copying the best ready-mades, a frustration has been trying to duplicate the flatlock-like stitch seen on swimsuit elastic applications, belt loops, and sportswear seams. **Labeled a cover or covering stitch,** it is produced by industrial machines that sew three times as fast as your home-use serger and look more like king-size conventional sewing machines. The stitch elements combine the two technologies, however; like sergers, the cover stitch machines have loopers which form the horizontal stitch elements. For instance, if the cover stitch is a 2-needle, 3-thread, then there's one looper (that passes catching the needle threads on the underside). The 2-needle, 4-thread stitch has two loopers that catch the two needle threads (one that passes over the

topside and one on the underside). See Fig. 2-1.

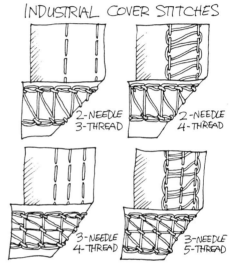

Fig. 2-1

A major difference between the industrial cover stitch and the stitch a serger produces is that **the cover stitch doesn't trim,** so butting, hemming, and seaming can be flat, without folding. Also, without knives, the cover stitch is not used for finishing of seam edges.

With a home-use serger, **the closest imitation of the 3-needle cover stitch is mock hemstitching,** developed by Naomi Baker. After flatlocking, topstitch from the wrong side through the center of the stitch with the same thread or invisible nylon thread in the bobbin (Fig. 2-2). (The next closest

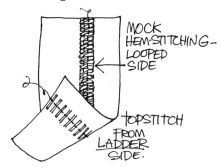

Fig. 2-2

cover-stitch look-alike is balanced tension flatlocking, explained on page 49.)

Faux Flatlocking

Ready-mades feature cover-stitched (see page 14) seam accents that add subtle same-color texture without being blatantly decorative. Faux flatlocking emulates cover-stitching but requires no special tension adjustments and is more durable than actual flat-locking.

• **Faux flatlock seams** with matching serger or all-purpose thread create detailing that doesn't shout "Decorative!" Worked on spongy interlock or fleece knits, the stitch buries beautifully in the fabric surface, becoming an integral part of the texture.

1. Thread the loopers and needle with matching all-purpose or serger thread. Adjust for a medium to wide width and medium length, balanced 3-thread stitch. Wind two bobbins of the same

thread for the top and bobbin of the conventional machine straight-stitching.

2. Serge the seams *wrong sides together* (Fig. 2-3).

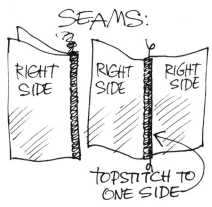

Fig. 2-3

3. Topstitch the serged seam to one side. (Be consistent throughout the garment in lapping direction. We usually lap all seams to the back.)

☞ **Update tip:** If melt adhesive thread (see page 140) such as Thread-Fuse™ is used in the lower looper, the serged seam can simply be pressed down. However, watch the direction of stitching, so that the melt adhesive thread is positioned on the side that will be pressed down.

• **Ribbing can be applied with faux flatlocking,** too (Fig. 2-4). The double-

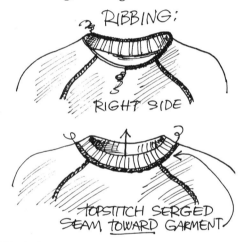

Fig. 2-4

stitched faux flatlocking stands up well to the stretching of openings.

• **For hemlines,** serge-finish the hem edge, press to the right side, and top-stitch. If using a fabric with definite right and wrong sides, forgo this

technique—just press up the hem to the wrong side and topstitch. See Fig. 2-5.

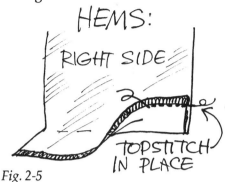

Fig. 2-5

• **For facings,** trim the facing width to 1 1/2"-2" (or as desired). With the facing right side up, serge-finish the edge. Serge the facing to the garment edge, *the right side of the facing to the wrong side of the garment.* (Serge-seaming the facing eliminates trimming and grading.) Press the facing to the right side and topstitch in place (see Fig. 2-6).

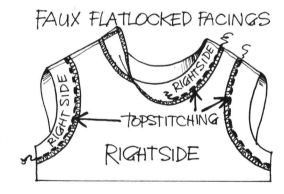

Fig. 2-6

Johnny Collars: An Easy Crew Combo

Johnny collars are everywhere-on sweats, on T-shirts, and even on dressier wool jerseys. The ribbed collar-crew band combo is more versatile and flattering than a plain crew (due to the built-in stand), yet takes only minutes more to sew. And the collar is convertible to a mock turtleneck; use buttons or a decorative pin to instantly wrap the casual collar up into the higher neckline.

Any crew neckline top can be quickly adapted—simply add a matching collar (the collar width should be at least twice that of the finished crew rib). If you can't find a perfect purchased collar match, sew a collar from ribbed yardage or self-fabric (Fig. 2-7). Think about contrasting colors for hard-to-match garment shades.

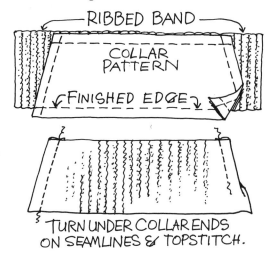

Fig. 2-7

To make a Johnny collar, follow these four simple steps:

1. Before seaming, narrow the garment neckline seam allowance (to about 1/4"-3/8") *if necessary.* You can vary the ribbing width as desired; it serves as a stand for your collar. (See *Creative Serging Illustrated* for ribbing application hints.) Using a medium-width and medium-length overlock stitch, apply the crew ribbing to the neckline (Fig. 2-8).

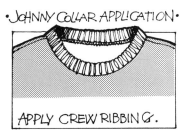

Fig. 2-8

2. Overlap the ends of the collar about 3/8" and machine baste. (For convertibility, *the edges should meet or overlap in the center front.*) See Fig. 2-9.

OVERLAP COLLAR 3/8".

Fig. 2-9

3. Pin the collar in place, the underside against the wrong side of the crew ribbing. Distribute the ease evenly (the collar will be stretched to fit the neckline). Match the collar overlap to the center front. See Fig. 2-10.

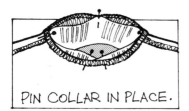

PIN COLLAR IN PLACE.

Fig. 2-10

4. **To apply the collar,** serge with the collar on top, starting at the center back. If possible, adjust the overlock stitch for a slightly wider width than was used to apply the crew ribbing; that way, the first row of serging will be completely covered. *Optional:* Edgestitch on the right side to secure all the seam layers toward the garment.

Variations: Convert to a stand-up collar by adding a button and buttonhole at the collar corners, as shown above. Try the garment on and mark correct placement before stitching. Buttonholes are generally on the right collar corner (for women and girls), stitched diagonally and corded to prevent stretching. Buttons are sewn on the underside of the left collar. Or, just use a fun pin to wrap and fasten the collar.

Modular Knit Know-How

Conceived originally by **Units System's** first designer, Sandra Garratt, the modular knit trend has taken Seventh Avenue by storm, spawning dozens of copycat brands. The sewing industry hasn't missed this fashion wave. Virtually every company now offers its own version of mix-and-match knit separates, for women and girls. Have a ball belting, wrapping, and layering the knit pieces into ingenious dressing arrangements.

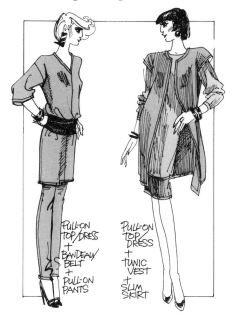

Pull-on Top/Dress + Bandeau Belt + Pull-on Pants

Pull-on Top/Dress + Tunic Vest + Slim Skirt

You simply won't believe how quickly these knit pieces can be seamed and edge-finished. Devoid of facings, fasteners, or inner construction, as many as three pieces can easily be completed in an evening of sewing. However, *you must use the fabrics suggested on the pattern envelope; knits like interlocks, double-knits, and some jerseys* that have 25-50% stretch and no discernible right or wrong side make the fast fitting, seaming, and finishing possible.

You have many seaming and finishing options (this also applies to hems). *The key is to coordinate the two, unifying the stitching accents throughout the garment.* Each option utilizes both conventional and serger sewing.

Option A.

Seams: Straight-stitch right sides together (1/2" to 3/4" allowances), serge together the allowances, and topstitch to one side.

Edges: Serge, turn under (about 1/2"), and topstitch with a single or twin needle (about 3/8" from the fold). See Fig. 2-11.

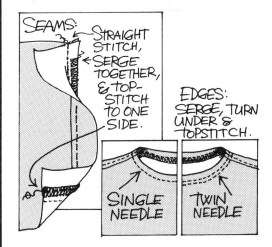

SEAMS: Straight Stitch, Serge Together, & Topstitch to one side.

EDGES: Serge, turn under & topstitch.

SINGLE NEEDLE   TWIN NEEDLE

Fig. 2-11

Option B.

Seams: Straight-stitch right sides together (1/2" to 3/4" seam allowances), press open, and topstitch 3/8" on either side of the seamline with straight or zigzag topstitching.

Edges: Serge, turn under (about 1/2"), and topstitch with straight or zigzag topstitching (about 3/8" from the fold). See Fig. 2-12.

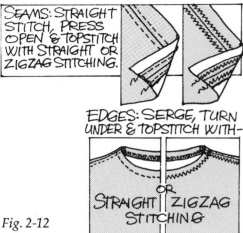

Fig. 2-12

☞ **Update tip:** Many of the ready-to-wear modular knits, like the **Units System,** use zigzag topstitching throughout; seams are not sewn or finished with serging. These companies obviously must struggle with labor costs; you can choose the optimum techniques for your fabric and the garment.

Option C.

Seams: Serge (right or wrong sides together), trimming the seam allowances. (If you've serged wrong sides together, we recommend edge-stitching the serged seam toward the back side of the garment.)

Edges: Serge, turn under to the wrong side (about 1/2"), and topstitch with a single or twin needle as in Option A. Or, serge, turn to the right side (about 1/2"), and edge-stitch along the needle line, as shown. See Fig. 2-13.

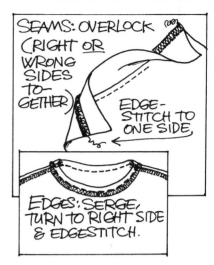

Fig. 2-13

Update on edge finishing: The serged, turned, and topstitched edges seen on modular knits are marvelously fast, flat, and functional. But some fabrics call for more finishing body and stability, particularly, at necklines. You'll love this beefy, more stable edge finish. Because the wrong side shows, self-binding is best for knits with no discernible wrong side. Also, maneuvering the serger foot is easiest around a more open, gradually curved neckline.

✎ **Note:** Allow a 7/8" allowance at the neckline edge.

1. Thread the needle and loopers with serger or all-purpose thread. Adjust for 5-mm wide, medium-length balanced 3-thread stitching.

2. Serge the shoulder seams *wrong sides together.* From the right side of the garment, topstitch the serged seam to the bodice back side of the seam.

3. Serge-finish the neckline edge.

4. Fold the serged edge 7/8" to the wrong side (Fig. 2-14).

Fig. 2-14

5. Serge along the fold (Fig. 2-15).

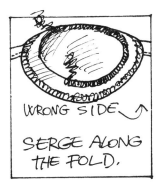

Fig. 2-15

6. Fold the serged edge about 3/8" over *to the right side* and edge-stitch, as shown (Fig. 2-16).

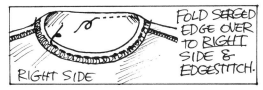

Fig. 2-16

Serge-Finished Ribbing

A new breed of ribbing has been appearing on sportswear everywhere. Close-up analysis reveals its humble beginnings: the ribbing edge has been serged rather than being folded or machine-finished. The result is single-layer ribbing that's less bulky and still the exact width needed; all you do is trim and serge-finish ribbed yardage or bands to the width desired.

1. Select ribbing yardage or bands that have enough body and resiliency to withstand the rigors of a single-layer application. Types that have worked well for us are fine-gauge cottons and cotton blends. Lycra®-cotton blends are perfect, if you can find them. (Avoid most acrylics; they lack the resiliency required.) Test by stretching a single layer crosswise.

2. Determine whether one or both of the crosswise edges will be serge-finished. Ribbing finished along both edges can be lapped *wrong side over the right side* of the garment edge and edge-stitched in place with a single or twin needle. Ribbing finished along one edge is seamed to the garment along the other edge, right sides together.

3. Adjust your machine for a wide, medium-to-long length 3/4-thread stitch. (If 3/4-thread stitching is not an option, use a wide 3-thread stitch.) Any matching or intentionally contrasting serger or all-purpose weight thread works well. Serge-finish the edge. See Fig. 2-17.

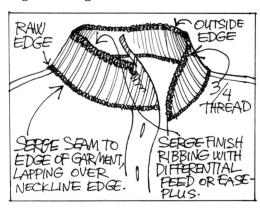

Fig. 2-17

If available, dial the differential feed knob to 2.0, a setting that should effectively ease the ribbing, preventing stretching and rippling. If your machine doesn't have differential feeding, simulate the action manually by force-feeding the ribbing under the foot and holding your forefinger behind the foot (see "ease-plus," page 108). Experiment with different stitch lengths to establish which setting produces the least

stretching, while still covering the edge adequately.

☞ **Update tip:** The hottest knits in sportswear tout stretched-out serged ribbing. So, if you or your kids are into the "expensive cool" look, don't worry about controlling the ribbing edge stretch.

Sleek Wraps: A Seventh Avenue Trend

Designers Donna Karan and Giorgio di Sant'Angelo have spearheaded what Seventh Avenue calls the "surplice," and you'll now see the flattering trend

copied in all the pattern books. The potential problem areas for homesewn wraps are choosing the wrong fabric choice and handling bulk. We offer some solutions:

If you've never sewn a wrap style before, **start with a knit.** Cotton or cotton-blend interlocks are nearly goof-proof fabrics, easy-to-serge, and readily available. If you prefer a lighter weight, consider jerseys. Lycra blends move with body-hugging wraps. Steer clear of any bulky fabric, and heed pattern envelope warnings about one-way prints or diagonals.

To decrease bulk wherever possible, replace facings with serged, turned, and topstitched edges. If additional stabilizing is called for at the neckline, try serging polyurethane "plastic" elastic to the wrong side of the edge before turning and topstitching (see page 11).

Rather than making double layer-faced ties, cut the ties slightly wider and serge-finish the edges single layer. Tightly constructed fabrics, like silky crepe de chine and some stable wool jerseys, can be simply serge-finished along the tie edges; knits and loosely constructed wovens should be serge-finished, turned, and topstitched, as shown in Fig. 2-18.

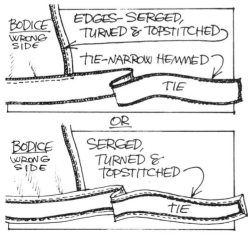

BODICE WRONG SIDE — EDGES- SERGED, TURNED & TOPSTITCHED — TIE-NARROW HEMMED — TIE

OR

BODICE WRONG SIDE — SERGED, TURNED & TOPSTITCHED — TIE

Fig. 2-18

✎ **Note:** For the sleekest wrapped fastening, *thread tie ends though a buckle,* rather than knotting.

Snazzy Serged Reversibles

Reversibles are getting star billing in the best stores and catalogs. It's no surprise that serging plays a supporting role; the lightweight, ravel-free finishing and seaming supersede the tedious flatfelling or stitch-and-turn schemes of sewing days past.

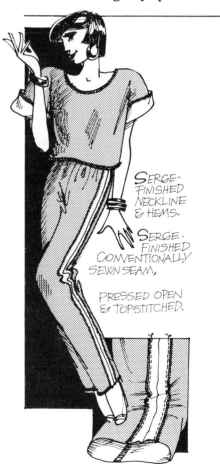

SERGE-FINISHED NECKLINE & HEMS.

SERGE-FINISHED CONVENTIONALLY SEWN SEAM,

PRESSED OPEN & TOPSTITCHED.

Faster, less bulky serging methods and luscious fabrics beckon even if you've never been tempted by reversibles before. Fabric inventories—double-faced denims, sportweight wovens, knits, and suitings—infuse creativity. Double-sided serge-finishing and seaming are perfect for these double-sided fabrics.

Or, you can replicate single-layer reversible fabric by combining two layers of contrasting color fabrics. Stick with light-to-medium weights so the finished garment won't be too heavy. A perfect project pick would be a silky reversible pant and top, made of two fabric layers throughout (an inspiration from a Bloomingdale's catalog). Not only can the outfit be worn on either side, multiplying the mingling and matching, but the self-lining adds body and wrinkle- resistance. Luckily, numerous patterns mirror the popular ready-to-wear versions nearly seam for seam. Sew a flared skirt (single layer) in either or both colors to create an office-right ensemble.

VERSATILE REVERSIBLES!

The outfit from Bloomingdale's was made of the wrinkled washable silk so trendy now and available in fabric stores, but silk or silky crepe de chine, faille, or charmeuse will work equally well. Note that real silks will stay rolled up into sleeve or pant cuffs better than slippery silkies. *Prelaunder the fabrics to prevent the darker shade from bleeding onto the lighter shade;* silk is famous for crocking, so nix red and white combos (you'd be safer with black and royal blue). Test by rubbing prewashed swatches together to check for dye transfer.

1. **Check fitting before cutting out.** *Essential to the look and successful layering of the two fabrics is a loose fit.* Straighten the blouse hem (eliminating shirttail curves and side slits) to facilitate continuous serging; alter to the most flattering length. Add an all-in-one paper-bag casing, as shown in Fig. 2-19. Even though serge-finishing will substitute for hems, leave hem allowances on and trim off after fitting.

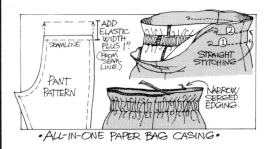

• ALL-IN-ONE PAPER BAG CASING •

Fig. 2-19

2. **Interface the neckline of one top layer.** Fuse a facing-sized piece of pre-shrunk *Easy-Knit* to the wrong side of the neckline edge.

3. With a standard-width and -length stitch, **serge to assemble each of the two top and two pant layers.** Start with a new size 9 or 11 (65/75) needle.

4. Slip one top inside the other top, *wrong sides together.* Do the same for the pants. Pin intermittently to secure the layers. Try on the outfit (it should fit easily over your head and hips) and **mark the length and layer inconsistencies; take off and trim along markings.** Fold the layers back and loosely hand-tack corresponding allowances at a few seam intersections to help keep the layers in alignment (tack the underarms, shoulder and sleeve, crotch).

5. **Adjust for narrow (either rolled or balanced), short satin serging.** Thread the loopers with woolly stretch nylon alone, or combine it in the upper looper with a fine rayon thread. Using two layers of the fabric scraps, test the stitch tension and length. *You may need to widen the bite width* (check your manual and see pages 136-137) for a cleaner, stronger edge. Reinforcing the neckline serging with straight stitching (along the needleline) is optional, but it is recommended for ravel-prone fabrics. For a wider rolled edge, serge-finish with the reversible binding stitch (see page 160).

6. **Serge the top edges, starting with the neckline. Serge slowly,** neatly overlapping the stitches for 1/2" or so,

at inconspicuous areas (see Fig. 2-20). Use a hand needle to weave the thread tails into the stitch. Serge in the directions shown so the edge finishing will be uniform on each side.

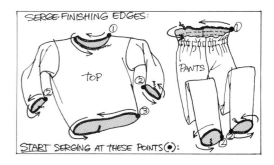

Fig. 2-20

☞ **Update tip:** If stretching during serge-finishing is a problem, lengthen your stitch and lighten the presser foot pressure. Also, try using knitting-in elastic (see page 31) in the needle to control stretch; test first on fabric scraps.

7. *Optional:* Turn the finished hem edges 1/2" to one side and edge-stitch, for durability and color contrast (Fig. 2-21).

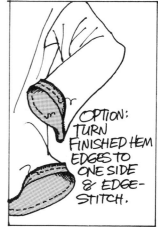

Fig. 2-21

8. With your conventional sewing machine, straight-stitch the lower casing line for the pant elastic application. Fit the elastic and zigzag into a circle; place between the wrong sides of the two layers. Straight-stitch the upper casing line. **Serge-finish the waistline ruffle with narrow edging,** trimming to even the layers. See Fig. 2-20.

9. **Try the pants on.** Mark the length and any layer inconsistencies; take off and trim along markings.

10. **Serge-finish the pant hem edge,** as you did the top hem. If you have turned and edge-stitched the blouse hems, do so here, too.

Crisscrossed Belt Loops

Besides liking the obvious waistline interest value of criss-crossed belt loops, you'll appreciate how well the crisscrossing holds belts ranging from narrow to wide. Serging the loop strip keeps bulk to a minimum.

1. Cut a straight-grain fabric strip 1-1/2" wide by the length needed. (You'll need 3-1/2" for each belt loop or 28" total for four sets of two.)

2. Serge-finish one side of the loop strip (Fig. 2-22).

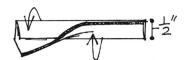

Fig. 2-22

3. Fold the loop strip as shown, right sides out (Fig. 2-23).

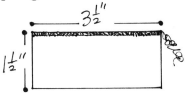

Fig. 2-23

4. From the right side, edge-stitch close to the edge folds.

5. Clip the loop strip into 3-1/2" pieces.

6. Press under 1/4" to the wrong side on each end of each loop piece. *Topstitch to the waistline* of the garment, angling the cross as shown or desired (Fig. 2-24). Fit to your favorite belt width.

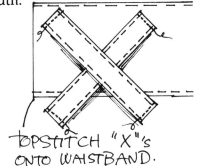

Fig. 2-24

Ready-to-Wear Elastic Applications

Clotilde Lampe (of Clotilde, Inc.), Nancy Zieman (of Nancy's Notions, Ltd.), and our other friends in the notions business tell us that elastics have become best-selling items. The popularity of elastics is undoubtedly related to the popularity of stretch-fabric fashion—knit separates, aerobic-wear, cycling garb, and swimsuits. Other factors contributing to the success of elastics are comfort, instant fit, and sewing speed.

When sewing knits or wovens, a growing number of busy seamsters rely on elastic applications to replace traditional (more time-consuming) waistbands, cuffs, and facings. Update your elastic know-how with our collection of new looks, products, and techniques, all borrowed from the latest ready-to-wear.

Exposed Elastic Bands

Apply exposed elastic bands to pull-on shorts, pants, and skirts. You'll be duplicating one of the hottest retail trends, while conveniently economizing on fabric and sewing time. Ruffled on one edge, the width varies from 2"-

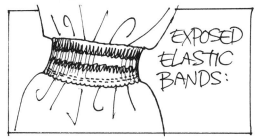

6". The popular 3" width is best suited to most larger-than-model-size waists.

1. Follow a flat construction order, if possible. Stitch all but one seam, so that the elastic can be applied flat. Quarter-mark the waistline.

2. Fit the elastic to your waist. (Wide elastic has a tendency to buckle when strained, so fit loosely.) Add 1" for seam allowances. Quarter-mark the elastic.

3. Along the waistline edge, serge over *(but not through)* heavy thread. Secure one end of the heavy thread by wrapping in a figure eight around a long pin. Pull the other end of the heavy thread to gather the edge. See Fig. 2-25.

Fig. 2-25

4. Lap the wrong side of the elastic 5/8" over the right side of the garment (to the seamline). Matching the quarter-marks, twin-needle topstitch the elastic to the waistline. See Fig. 2-26.

Fig. 2-26

5. Straight-stitch the remaining seam, through the elastic. Backstitch. Top-stitch the elastic seam allowances on both sides of the seamline.

The Two-Step Topstitched Casing

This elastic casing method is the one technique preferred by most active-wear manufacturers. Rather than being inserted through a casing, the elastic is sewn to the wrong side of the opening edge, then turned to the inside and topstitched from the right side. Twisting of the elastic is eliminated, and distribution of ease is stitched in, permanently. Use it to finish and contour edges on stretch fashions—swimsuits, leotards, tights, or any tight-fitting knit separates.

☞ **Update tip:** Some sergers have an elastic application foot handy for unseamed applications (see page 140); a screw on the top of the foot automatically adjusts the stretch of the elastic as it is applied. Test to gauge the stretch adjustment.

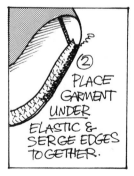

1. Cut the elastic according to the pattern instructions or ratio/measurement guidelines. Quarter-mark both the elastic and opening. Adjust your serger for a long, medium-width stitch; serge several stitches in one end of the elastic to anchor the stitching. See Fig. 2-27. (You can also seam the elastic in a circle before applying, but we find unseamed elastic much easier to serge accurately.)

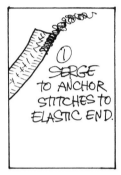

Fig. 2-27

2. Place the *wrong side of garment* opening under the elastic and serge, stretching only the elastic and matching quarter-markings (Fig. 2-28).

Fig. 2-28

3. Lap the elastic ends 1/2" and serge, overlapping the previous stitching to secure. Serge off the edge. See Fig. 2-29.

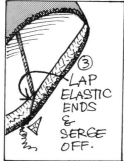

Fig. 2-29

5. Turn the elastic to the wrong side, encasing it. Topstitch conventionally from the right side to secure all layers, using one of three options:

• **With a long, straight-stitch** (8 spi), topstitch from the right side. (When using 3/8"-wide elastic, stitch about 1/4" from folded edge.) Stretch the edge firmly while topstitching. See Fig. 2-30.

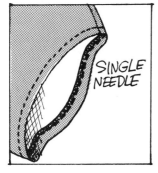

Fig. 2-30

• **With a twin needle** and a long, straight-stitch (8 spi), topstitch from the right side. (The underside is a zigzag stitch, as shown.) Although this is a stretchier stitch, stretching while stitching is still required. See Fig. 2-31.

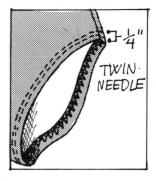

Fig. 2-31

• **With a wide, medium-length zigzag stitch,** stitch over the serge-finished edge from the wrong side. Hold fabric taut or stretch slightly while stitching. See Fig. 2-32.

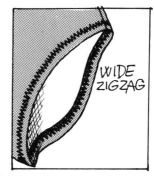

Fig. 2-32

Elasticized Binding

Another ready-to-wear application, elasticized binding, stabilizes an edge and also serves as a decorative finish. (The binding can also extend into straps.) Finishing is neat, on the inside of the garment or the underside of the strap.

1. Cut the trim strip and elastic, as shown in Fig. 2-33. (The greatest stretch should parallel the length of the strap.)

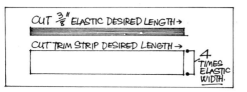

Fig. 2-33

2. Match cut edges of trim strip and garment, right sides together. Straight-stitch the strip to garment, using a 3/8" seam allowance. *Stretch both layers as you sew.* See Fig. 2-34.

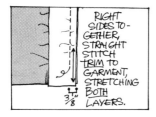

Fig. 2-34

3. Adjust the serger for a long, medium-width 3-thread stitch. Serge the

elastic to the seam allowance through all layers. See Fig. 2-35. Be careful not to cut the elastic.

Fig. 2-35

4. Fold strip 3/8" to wrong side, matching the cut edge to the serged edges. Fold 3/8" again, encasing the elastic. See Fig. 2-36.

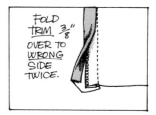

Fig. 2-36

5. With the right side up, twin needle topstitch to secure the binding layers (Fig. 2-37).

Fig. 2-37

Elastic Shirring

Study the shirring so common in ready-to-wear. You'll notice it is a serged chainstitch. (If you're uncertain whether your serger chainstitches, ask your dealer. All 4/2-thread and many 5-thread models do.)

Use elastic thread in the looper of a 2-thread chainstitch to create the shirring on lighter-weight fabrics such as tricots, single-knit jerseys, and woven sheers. (To shirr, you must be able to disengage the upper looper and the movable knife.) Start by loosening the looper tension, then tighten incrementally for more gathering. Lengthening the stitch will also increase the shirring. With the right side of the fabric on top, serge chainstitching rows about a presser-foot's width apart. See Fig. 2-38.

The width of the shirred section will be limited by the amount of room to the right of the needle, which varies from one serger brand to another. (One serger model has no obstacles to the right of the needle, allowing chainstitched topstitching anywhere on the project.) Knitting-in elastic can also be used for shirring tricots and sheers; however, our favorite use of this much finer elastic is in the needle of serged edging to control stretching.

If your serger doesn't chainstitch, fold the fabric right sides together and serge-seam over elastic cord. Pull the elastic to shirr. See Fig. 2-39. If this method creates too much bulk, try folding the fabric right sides together and flatlocking (see page 159) over elastic cord. Pull the flatlocking flat, and then pull the elastic cord to shirr.

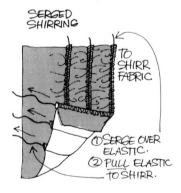

Fig. 2-39

Fig. 2-38

3. Yes, You Can Serge Jackets and Coats

Serging can replace or complement traditional tailoring methods. Exposed facing and seam edges in unlined and partially lined jackets can be beautifully and quickly finished. Even a fully lined jacket or coat can be serged in strategic areas to speed assembly, finish with less bulk, and add durability. And, decorative serging is a natural for finishing facingless edges on boiled-wool jackets and double-faced coatings. Go for it. With a serger, you'll actually complete your jacket before it's out of season or style.

Speediest Serged Tailoring

Speed tailoring has rescued many trapped in the sewing catch-22: New roles demand professional clothes while fragmenting the time to sew them. Due to this dilemma, speed tailoring has become the popular approach to making jackets and coats; tedious pad-stitched shaping is replicated by fast, fusible interfacings. With your serger and the following tips, this process can be speedier than ever.

• *For unlined jackets,* or those made of fabric that is bulky or that ravels badly, **serge the raw edges of the major garment seams,** as shown in Fig. 3-1, after

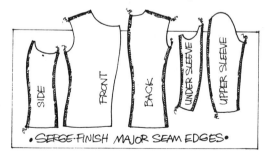

Fig. 3-1

removing the pattern pieces. Be careful to skim (not trim) the edges to maintain accurate seam width later. Serging preserves the piece size and shape during fitting and sewing. And it's always easier to serge-finish before straight-stitching seams.

If you've mastered serge-seaming along 5/8" seam allowances, **consider serging major lengthwise jacket seams.** (Serging seams is not recommended, however, for bulky fabrics or when fit is uncertain.) Use a 4- or 5-thread stitch, if available, for the strongest, most stable seams. Press serged seams to one side, being careful to avoid seam imprinting on the right side. Use traditional straight-stitched, pressed-open seams at the shoulders to minimize bulk and stretching.

• **Serge the facing shoulder seams** and press to one side. See Fig. 3-2.

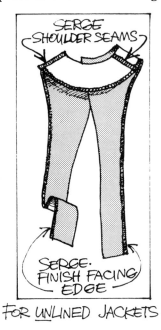

Fig. 3-2

In unlined jackets, **serge the outer facing edge** for a beautifully flat finish. *For lined jackets,* **serge the bottom 3" on the outer edge of the facing** for a neat, unbulky finish where the facing overlaps the jacket hem below the lining. Gradually taper on and off the facing edge, just skimming the edge to finish. See Fig. 3-3.

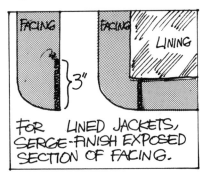

Fig. 3-3

• **Assemble the lining bodice on the serger.** Then serge the completed lining to the facing. Angle the serging on and off the seam allowance 6" from the bottom edges, as shown in Fig. 3-4.

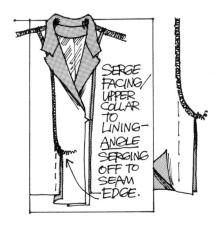

Fig. 3-4

• Straight-stitch the upper collar/facing unit and the undercollar/jacket unit together to complete. Press.

• **Assemble the sleeve linings on the serger** and press the seams to one side. Serge the sleeve lining hem edge right sides together to the jacket sleeve hem edge. To anchor the hem on two-piece jacket sleeves, simply stitch-in-the-ditch of the hem seamlines; stitch from the right side for accuracy. *On jackets with one-piece sleeves*, hand-catch-stitch the sleeve hem after serging the lining to the edge.

• **Set the sleeves in with straight-stitching.** Ensure a custom fit by setting the sleeve lining into the lining armhole by hand, as is done in traditional tailoring. (Use two strands of waxed thread and hand-felling stitches.)

• *For unlined pockets*, **serge-finish the pocket edges** (Fig. 3-5). Or, for quick

lining and stabilizing, fuse Easy-Knit fusible tricot interfacing to the wrong side of the pocket before serge-finishing. Complete and attach pockets following the pattern directions.

• The same serging techniques apply to **tailored coats.** After hemming the completed coat, hem the lining shorter. **Serge-finish the lining raw edge. Use serged thread chains as swing tacks** to secure the lining to the coat hem, as shown in Fig. 3-6.

Fig. 3-6

Adjust for a rolled-edge finish and use polyester topstitching thread in the loopers. Holding the thread tails tightly, serge a continuous chain several inches long for each swing tack needed. Thread the unchained thread ends into a large-eyed needle and sew to the lining hem allowance with several small stitches. Thread the remaining end of the serger chain into a needle and stitch to the coat hem, making a 1" swing tack. See Fig. 3-6.

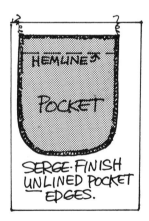

Fig. 3-5

Soft Tailoring: Savvy Serging Strategies

Soft-tailored jackets make fashion and sewing sense. The look is now and versatile; the unlined silhouette can be worn open and free-flowing or shaped with wrapping and a belt. Construction is incredibly fast; apply tandem technology (straight-stitching and serging) and this savvy sewing order to complete a jacket, easily, in just one evening session.

1. **Straight-stitch** the shoulder seams of the jacket and facings. **Press** the facing seams open.

2. **Serge-finish** the seam and facing edges, as shown in Fig. 3-7.

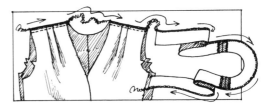

Fig. 3-7

3. **Serge** the facing to the jacket. Turn and press.

4. **Serge** the pocket pieces to the front and back side seams (Fig. 3-8).

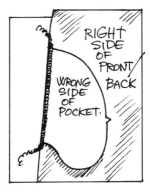

Fig. 3-8

5. **Straight-stitch** the side seams. Serge-finish the seam edges together. Press the seams and pockets toward the center front (Fig. 3-9).

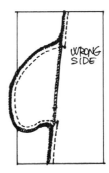

Fig. 3-9

6. **Serge-finish** the jacket and sleeve hems (Fig. 3-10).

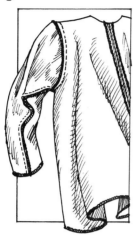

Fig. 3-10

7. **Straight-stitch** the sleeves to the jacket. Serge-finish the seam edges together. See Fig. 3-10.

☞ **Update tip:** Spoil yourself with other soft-tailoring strategies. For example, on this flared jacket, serge the band (a rectangular strip folded lengthwise, wrong sides together) to the already hemmed jacket. Wear the collar rolled back or turned up. See Fig. 3-11a and b.

SERGE FOLDED SELF-FABRIC BAND TO THE HEMMED JACKET.

Fig. 3-11a

TECHNIQUE FOCUS: EASY FRONT BAND

Fig. 3-11b

Serging Boiled Wool (Beautifully)

Discount ready-to-wear catalogs now promote "boiled wool" jackets for as low as $100. Yet for the home sewer, the boiled-wool fabric notions and pattern can total nearly $90.

YARN SERGED EDGES.

So, why sew? "For superior fabric," claims Susan Schlief, a former *Sew News* editor and currently owner of Classic Cloth, a mail-order service and retail store specializing in boiled wool (see "Serge-by-Mail Directory," pages 163-173). "The authentic jackets made by *Geiger of Austria*, that retail for $160 to $200, are actually made of a boiled-wool knit, not a woven. The knit fits, drapes, and moves more fluidly and, fortunately, is easier to sew. Landau boiled wool, which we carry, is Austrian and knitted."

Whether you're buying a garment or sewing, *make note of the differences in the boiled wool available.* "Most of our customers decide the higher price ($48 to $56/yd.) of the knitted, imported fabric is well worth it," according to Susan.

Another enticement of boiled wool is the speed at which it can be sewn and serged. Preshrunk at high temperatures to compact the fibers, this fabric offers the benefits of fast, unlined construction without sacrificing quality. Ravel-free with body galore, boiled wool serges and sews beautifully single layer, sans facings, interfacings, and linings. An evening of sewing will produce a comfortable classic that will endure through season after season of unpredictable fashion changes.

☞ **Update tip:** Ironically, this preshrunk fabric will shrink more. Pretreat the fabric (and trims, if applicable) as you would the finished garment: Steam well if dry cleaning (our preference) or hand wash in tepid water and lay out flat to dry.

Patterns: Minimizing Yardage and Sewing Time

Some patterns have been specifically designed for boiled wool or felted fabrics that perform similarly. You'll recognize them by the Tyrolean styling and listing of boiled wool under "Suggested Fabrics" on the pattern catalog page and envelope.

Shorter, collarless styles will cut yardage requirements and sewing time, plus they will more closely resemble the ready-made jackets. Look for interpretations of the classic buttoned-front cardigan, perhaps updated with a flared back hem. If your fashion sights are set on a longer jacket with lapels, there are several styles shown in the pattern books. (For jackets with lapels, follow the sewing order given for "Gail's Five-step Jacket" on page 60 of *Creative Serging Illustrated* rather than steps presented below.) A few are designed to be worn buttonless and belted, so buttonhole making is eliminated.

☞ **Update tip:** Most knitted boiled wool will cost from $40-60 per yard, so careful calculation of yardage requirements is essential. Using only the front, back, sleeve, and front pocket (optional) pattern pieces, plan a layout on a cutting board, using 52-54" fabric. For a basic jacket you may need as little as 1-1/4 yard, up to 1-3/4 yard for more detailed, longer designs. *Take preshrinking into account;* after pretreating, 1-1/2 yards by 60" wide will be about 1-1/4 yards by 52-54".

To make a jacket, follow these sewing and serging how-to's:

1. **Staystitch (with straight-stitching) along neckline and hem edges** to prevent stretching. You may need to "ease plus" as you straight-stitch to control edge stretch.

2. **Straight-stitch the shoulder seams** and press open (this will be less bulky than serged seams). In keeping with

Austrian tradition, topstitch the seam 1/4" on either side of the seamline. See Fig. 3-12.

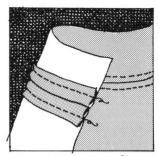

STRAIGHT STITCH, PRESS OPEN & TOPSTITCH SEAM ALLOWANCES.

Fig. 3-12

3. On boiled-wool fabric scraps, **practice serge-finishing** with baby or sport-weight yarn in the upper and lower looper and matching serger thread in the needle. The widest stitch setting looks best and minimizes stretching. Experiment with the stitch length; if the stitch is too short, jamming and stretching are inevitable. Of course, *tension must be very loose on the upper and lower loopers* to accommodate the yarn, which may mean removing the yarn from the tension dials completely. For extra edge stability, cord the serging with a yarn strand.

Your stitch-testing will be time well spent. *Substituting a decoratively serged yarn (at $3 per skein or so) for the more typical wool braid will save you $15-$20 in braid expenses.*

Note: Having trouble using yarn in the lower looper? This may be due to the size of your serger's lower looper eye (which varies from brand to brand). If, after repeated trials, you are still unsuccessful, use serger thread in the lower (this is not recommended, however, if the jacket has a roll line, because the stitch will no longer be reversible). Another decorative stitch alternative is reversible edge binding (see pg. 160); use yarn in the upper looper only and serger or all-purpose thread in the needle and lower looper.

4. **Serge-finish the neckline, front, and hem edges** of the jacket pieces, as shown in Fig. 3-13.

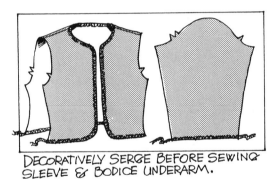

DECORATIVELY SERGE BEFORE SEWING SLEEVE & BODICE UNDERARM.

Fig. 3-13

5. **Set in the sleeves with straight-stitching.** Trim or serge off the seam to about 3/8" and press lightly toward the sleeve.

6. **Sew the sleeve and bodice under-arm seams,** as illustrated for the shoulder seams. *For perfect edge matching,* start at the bodice and sleeve hems, stitching to meet at the armhole/sleeve seam. Press open and topstitch. Trim and secure yarn tails.

7. **Try on the jacket and mark the buttons/buttonholes.** *Important:* cord buttonholes to prevent stretching. *Optional:* Make matching shoulder pads out of two layers of boiled wool. For a thicker pad, sandwich a layer or layers of polyester fleece between the fabric layers. Serge the curved edges together. Hand-tack in place after pin fitting.

Sources: Check with your local fabric retailers. Also, contact Classic Cloth, Clearbrook Woolen Shop, and G Street Fabrics. (For addresses, see "Serge-by-Mail Directory," pages 163-173.)

4. The Newest Decorative Threads, Techniques, & Stitches

Between the finishing of *Creative Serging Illustrated* and the writing of this book, many new and exciting threads suitable for serging have been introduced. Your embellishment options have never been so varied or serger-compatible.

The Latest on Threads

• We've been serge-testing a revolutionary new product, **a melt adhesive thread called *ThreadFuse*™**, and the results are newsworthy. Made of polyester, the loosely twisted thread has a heat-activated fusible component. The thread doesn't disappear, but the fusible component, when melted with pressing, forms a bond without weakening the thread.

Both practical and creative applications for melt adhesive thread abound. Threaded in the lower looper when serge-seaming, it allows the seaming to be neatly pressed to one side (eliminating edge-stitching that shows on the right side). Or it can be threaded in the upper looper and used to serge-finish an edge; trim or any overlay can be lapped and pressed to the edge, eliminating securing with gluing or topstitching. When you make couching braid with melt adhesive thread in the lower looper thread, the braid can be effortlessly pressed to the shape of the motif before being stitched down (see page 60).

Because the adhesive is integral to the stitches, it is always uniform and lightweight, making it safer than potentially globby glues. Undoubtedly, there are dozens of other practical applications—in serging and conventionally sewing—for this innovative thread development. We are continuing our testing. *ThreadFuse*™, distributed exclusively by The Perfect Notion (see page 167), is costly (almost $50 for a 2550-yard cone), but that quantity should last several months.

When this book went to press, no other melt adhesive thread besides the *ThreadFuse*™ brand had been brought to our attention. But the thread is so nifty, we felt it was just a matter of time before this brand would be more widely distributed or other similar melt adhesive brands were sold. Be on the lookout.

• **Monofilament nylon thread,** particularly the fine size 80, has been discovered of late by home sewers. It's handy as an element in many decorative applications and for delicate rolled hemming that blends with any color fabric. See the examples on page 51.

• **Six-strand cotton embroidery floss** has been readily available but not in a usable form for decorative serging (8- to 11-yard skeins). Madeira now offers the floss on 228-yard reels in dozens of colors. Made of long-staple colorfast cotton, it has a silky hand and sheen. The floss serges beautifully; the reel can feed directly into the serger. Loosen the upper looper enough to allow coverage of the fabric edge.

• **Untwisted rayon cord,** such as Madeira's *Decor 6,* is another decorative thread worth mentioning. This lustrous cording feeds easily through the ma-
chine. It is available on a 210-yard reel in 36 colors. Use in the upper looper tension guide; loosen the tension. *Decor 6* reportedly works well for decorative sewing machine embroidery, too; wind on the bobbin and bypass the tension slot in the bobbin holder.

• **Braided, flexible ribbon** is much easier to serge than are more stable, woven ribbons. If you've had trouble serging ribbons before, try this new product; it will remind you of the *Tinsel Twill* ribbon (see page 42). The width is about 1/8", and the color range is excellent—solids, metallics, and opalescents. The *Ribbon Thread* brand is distributed by Metier de Geneve and comes crosswound on 100-meter spools; it is sold by Elna dealers and other retailers. A similar product, called *Ribbon Floss,* is manufactured and distributed by Rhode Island Textile, the elastics specialist. Sold on 40-yard spools, it will be available through fabric stores, dealers, and from mail-order sources like Nancy's Notions.

• **Heavier, twisted rayon threads** look like #8 pearl cotton, but they are shinier and more tightly twisted. *Pearl Crown Rayon* is the brand offered by YLI; it serges beautifully.

• **Glass bead trim** is an unusual decorative product that's been turning heads. Small glass beads are crosslocked together with an interlocking chain of cotton threads. Distributed by International Bead and Sequin, *Crosslocked Glass Bead Trim* is both washable and drycleanable. Apply with a rolled edge (Fig. 4-1) or flatlocking as instructed in "Serging Bead Strands," pages 63-64.

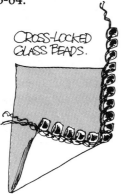

CROSS-LOCKED GLASS BEADS.

Fig. 4-1

• **Woolly stretch nylon threads** (our umbrella term for texturized nylon threads) have been around for some time, but there's still a lot of confusion about them. Because the thread is nylon, it makes a very strong seam. Instead of being twisted, the multifilaments are unplied, so they fluff to fill in the stitch (great for the upper looper of rolled edges) and create a soft edge or seam.

There are several brands of woolly stretch nylon now available: *Woolly Nylon*, the original from YLI; *Bulky Lock*, from Coats & Clark; *Metroflock*, from Swiss-Metrosene; Corticelli's *S-T-R-E-T-C-H-Y Nylon Thread*; and Talon's *Designer Edge*. All come on large crosswound spools or cones (averaging 1,100 yards) that can be placed directly on the serger thread rod.

✎ **Note:** As a general rule, *serger tensions must be loosened when using this thread*. Woolly stretch nylon can be used in the loopers and needle(s); if used in the needle on tight-fitting, two-way stretch fashions, it eliminates seam popping. (Keep stitches long, or this strong thread might cut the fibers.) Use woolly stretch nylon in the lower looper of a rolled-edge stitch to enhance tightening of the tension and, hence, rolling of the edge.

• **Several new metallic threads** work well for serging—*Twilley's Goldfingering*, *Gold Dust 20* (Fig. 4-2), and *Tinsel*

TWILLEY'S GOLD DUST 20 OR HEAVIER WEIGHT GOLDFINGER.

Fig. 4-2

Twill Ribbon. When serging with any of these metallics in the upper looper, it is a prerequisite that tensions be loosened. *Goldfingering*, in fact, requires bypassing the tension dial and hand-reeling. **Bonuses:** All three threads come in a wide range of colors, are washable in lukewarm water, are non-tarnishable, and are readily available.

Nomis' Together and *Angel's Hair* (Fig. 4-3) are finer metallic threads that can be combined in the upper looper

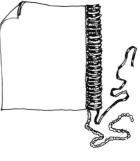

NOMIS ANGEL HAIR & WOOLLY STRETCH NYLON USED TOGETHER IN UPPER LOOPER.

Fig. 4-3

with threads like woolly stretch nylon or rayon, or with yarns. Again, both come in a range of colors. *Together* is solid-colored; *Angel's Hair* is multicolored.

A decorative wool-like yarn that serges smoothly is Madeira's *Burmilana #3*. The fine yarn is 30% wool and 70% acrylic. Washable in cool water, it can also be drycleaned. Available in 20 solid shades and 20 metallics, *Burmilana* is a real find.

Another easy-to-use entry in this category is *Sulky Metallic*. It is a polyester core thread available on 165-yard crosswound spools in twelve colors.

☞ **Update tip:** For better stitch coverage and durability, *combine a strand of woolly stretch nylon with metallic or rayon decorative thread* (usually in the upper looper). Tie both strands to the thread already in the machine and pull through the guides and eyes carefully. Place the smaller cone or spool on the thread rod and the woolly stretch nylon behind the machine. Use all-purpose or serger thread in the needle and woolly nylon in the lower looper. Adjust for narrow rolled or balanced hemming, and fine-tune the stitch length. Watch to make sure that both threads feed smoothly.

Sources: Check with your local fabric, yarn, and machine retailers, or try mail-order firms, such as Aardvark Adventures, Clotilde, Elsie's Exquisiques, Nancy's Notions, Speed Stitch, The Perfect Notion, Treadleart, and YLI. (For addresses, see "Serge-by-Mail Directory," page 166-168.)

The Latest Decorative Techniques

Your serger has capabilities far greater than everyday seaming and edge finishing. If you haven't tried using decorative threads, yarns, or ribbons, ready yourself for some fun—and some occasional frustration. Actually, the biggest obstacle to your decorative serging success may be finding the right threads, yarns, and ribbons. But you'll discover a surprising number of decorative possibilities at craft, needlework, and yarn shops and also at sewing machine dealerships specializing in machine embroidery.

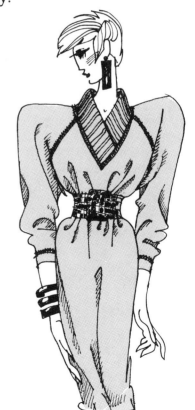

Not all decorative threads will feed smoothly through a serger. (Each serger brand and its respective models handle threads differently, some better than others.) Look for these weight, strength, pliability, and texture qualities:

• A single strand **should be fine enough to be threaded easily through the eye of the upper looper.** (The size of the upper looper eye varies, serger to serger.)

• The thread or yarn **should be twisted or braided tightly enough to prevent tangling in the loopers.** Loosely twisted yarns or threads tend to fray while passing through the looper eye. (Woolly stretch nylon is an exception, because it narrows to a finer strand as it feeds through the machine guides and tension adjustments.)

• Yarn and ribbon, in particular, **should be pliable enough to form the loops** fundamental to stitch formation. Plus, it should feed smoothly through the guides and eye(s). To test the pliability (and size), try threading a two-strand loop through the upper looper eye; if you have difficulty forming the loop or fitting it through the eye, the yarn or ribbon may be too stiff and/or wide to serge smoothly.

Decorative Serging: Ten Steps to Success

1. Allow at least eight yards of decorative thread for testing stitch width, length, and tensions, in addition to what you need for the project.

2. Start by threading the decorative thread *through the upper looper only*. (Most, but not all, applications feature the decorative thread in the upper looper only.) The upper looper has the least amount of stress on the thread.

☞ **Update tip:** If you'd prefer that the stitch look the same on both sides, adjust the tensions for reversible edge binding (see page 160). The upper looper will wrap completely around the edge.

3. Tie the decorative thread onto the all-purpose or serger-weight thread. Bypass the tension disks or dials; the knot can break when passing through. If necessary, cut the knot at the eye of the upper looper. Make a "thread cradle" (see page 34 of *Creative Serging Illustrated*) or use a fine wire needle threader (Fig. 4-4). After threading the eye, engage the decorative thread strand through the tension disk or dial.

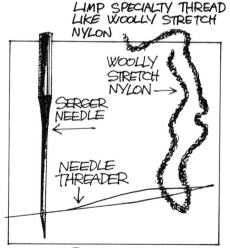

LIMP SPECIALTY THREAD
LIKE WOOLLY STRETCH
NYLON

WOOLLY
STRETCH
NYLON →

SERGER
NEEDLE
←

NEEDLE
THREADER
↓

FINE WIRE
NEEDLE THREADER

Fig. 4-4

4. Use matching all-purpose or serger-weight thread in the needle and lower looper. Or, substitute lightweight (#80) monofilament thread to create the illusion of floating the upper looper.

5. Adjust the stitch settings for wide, long serging. (The length can be shortened in stages if necessary.) Before beginning to serge, *turn the handwheel to ensure smooth feeding and correct stitch formation.* For the most accurate test, use scraps of the actual project fabric, optimally cut on the same grain as the edge to be finished.

6. *The heavier the thread, yarn, or ribbon, the looser the upper looper tension must be.* Metallic threads usually require looser tension than very smooth thread, such as rayon, so, the more resistance the thread, yarn, or ribbon exerts when passing through the tension guides, dials, and eyes, the more loosening they will require.

☞ **Update tip:** If the upper looper looks too tight or lacks uniformity and balance, more tension loosening may be required. For additional loosening of the loopers, first try skipping the holes in the thread guide plate or removing them from the pincher guide (Fig. 4-5). (These are the guides on the

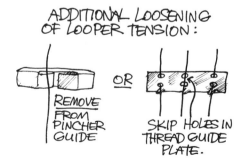

Fig. 4-5

front, directly below the telescoping thread stand.) If more loosening is needed, remove the strand from the tension dial (Fig. 4-6).

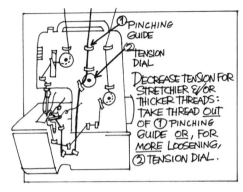

Fig. 4-6

7. Adjust the stitch length for the desired thread coverage. *The finer the thread, the shorter the stitch length.* Heavier yarns and ribbons demand a stitch length of at least 3 mm, and usually require more like 5 mm. As the stitch length is shortened, the tension will need to be tightened. Make adjustments by serging a few stitches at a time, then checking the stitch quality. Adjust, serge, and so on.

8. Try to achieve a uniform stitch that lies flat on the fabric surface. The lower looper tension should be adjusted so that it pulls the upper looper thread to the fabric edge (Fig. 4-7). If it

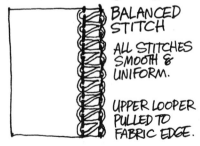

Fig. 4-7

doesn't, loosen the upper looper tension more and/or tighten the lower looper tension.

9. If the stitch width is uneven, narrowing intermittently (Fig. 4-8), the thread is not flowing freely. Reel off a few yards from the spool, cone, or ball; keep reeling as you serge slowly.

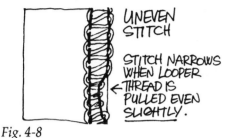

UNEVEN STITCH

STITCH NARROWS WHEN LOOPER ←THREAD IS PULLED EVEN SLIGHTLY.

Fig. 4-8

10. **Don't discard threads, ribbons, or yarns that your serger can't handle.** Instead, attempt to serge over one or more strands with a wide balanced or flatlock stitch.

☞ **Update tip:** When stitching over threads, yarns, or ribbons, the stitch width should be adjusted wide enough to serge over, rather than through them (Fig. 4-9). *Heavy threads, yarns, and flat*

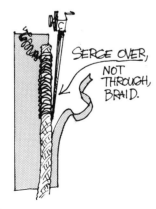

SERGE OVER, NOT THROUGH, BRAID.

Fig. 4-9

trims can be placed under the back of and over the front of the foot, to the right of the needle and left of the knife. Most standard serger feet have a right-hand front ledge; *if the strand is butted against the left side of the foot ledge, it will be automatically guided, cut-free, between the needle and knife.* See Fig. 4-10. *If the*

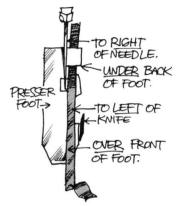

PRESSER FOOT→

—TO RIGHT OF NEEDLE.

←UNDER BACK OF FOOT.

←TO LEFT OF KNIFE

—OVER FRONT OF FOOT.

Fig. 4-10

strand is rounded and bulky (like heavy cording or a bead strand), the foot may need to be removed; hold the strand tight. (Consult "Neat Feet," pages 139-142, for slotted, bead strand, and piping applicator feet that are specially designed to accommodate bulky strands.)

How Will Decorative Serging Look on Your Garment?

• Every seam or edge has potential. Hems, necklines, yokes, pockets, plackets, collars, and ruffles can be decoratively serged. **Look for unusual design lines** to accentuate, or create design lines and motifs on the garment fabric with flatlocked topstitching (see page 159), serged appliqués (see page 64), or couching (see pages 57-60).

HIGHLIGHT DECORATIVE SERGING FIRST, RIGHT ON THE PATTERN ENVELOPE.

• Make a photocopy, tracing, or rough outline of the pattern view and **use colored pencils or felt-tip markers to highlight** your ideas for decorative serging. It's easy to preview the finished project; this highlighting also often reveals some unexpected figure-flattering (or not-so-flattering) illusions.

• **Don't dilute the design focus** by using decorative finishing in every possible area. (Go crazy with decorative serging on a pillow or belt, instead.) Odds are good that a garment outlined only at the neckline will be a winner. Follow two general rules here:

1. The simpler the pattern and the fabric, the more decorative serging can be used.

2. If in doubt, *leave it off.*

• **ALWAYS test-serge the decorative thread on your actual garment fabric.** (You may opt for the plain, all-purpose thread, stitched decoratively.)

The Latest Stitches: 3/4-Thread Innovations

If you think you've seen all the serger stitch possibilities, think again. Here are some brand-new stitch innovations developed in the Baby Lock sewing labs. You can try these stitches on any serger with 3/4-thread safety stitch capability.

• The **new tuck-and-roll stitch** is an adaptation of the 3/4-thread safety or mock safety stitch (see page 198). Converting this stitch to a narrow rolled edge normally requires removing the left needle and using only the right needle. But for this technique, simply leave both needles in place, making all the other adjustments for rolled-edge hemming (tightening of the lower looper thread is important). If your machine uses a different needle plate for the narrow rolled hem, be sure it has a hole for the left needle to enter unobstructed.

As the stitches form, *the tightened lower looper tension causes a tuck to form between the left needleline and the rolled edge* (see Fig. 4-11). This tuck-and-roll

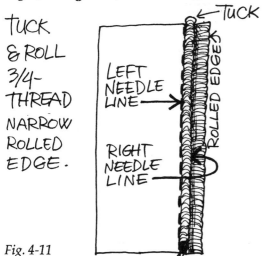

TUCK
& ROLL
3/4-
THREAD
NARROW
ROLLED
EDGE.

LEFT NEEDLE LINE →

RIGHT NEEDLE LINE

← TUCK

ROLLED EDGE

Fig. 4-11

combination can be used to finish an edge (trim at least slightly) or as a tuck (stitch on the fold, being careful not to nick it with the knife).

☞ **Update tip:** For a wider tuck-and-roll stitch, don't convert to narrow rolled-edge hemming. Keep your serger on standard 3/4-thread settings, but tighten the lower looper considerably (enough to form the tuck).

• The 3/4-thread safety stitch can also be used for flatlocking. This **3/4-thread flatlocking** is nearly identical to the stitch seen on ready-made active-wear—sweats, T-shirts, swimsuits, leotards, and tights, and it's easy. Begin with the basic 3/4-thread safety stitch,

3/4- THREAD FLAT- LOCKING

on the widest setting. Adjust the tensions, progressively tightening the lower looper and loosening the needle threads (so that the stitch will lie flat when pulled). Like the sample illustrated in Fig. 4-12, the 3/4-thread flat-

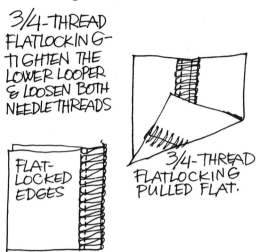

Fig. 4-12

locking has the additional right needleline running through the loop side of the stitch (the ladder side looks the same as 3-thread flatlocking). Make the stitch more pronounced by using heavier thread, yarn, or ribbon in the upper looper.

☞ **Update tip:** Overlock expert Ervena Yu teaches a 3-thread flatlock variation worth mentioning. *Maintain a balanced tension between the upper and lower looper* (rather than tightening down the lower looper). Loosen the needle tension as usual, so that the stitch will flatten when pulled. Keep playing with the tensions until the upper and lower looper threads inter-

lock in the middle of the stitch, as shown in Fig. 4--13. After you've mas-

Fig. 4-13

tered this stitch, experiment with using different thread shades in the upper and lower loopers to create an interesting multicolored stitch.

Flatter Flatlocking

✎ **Note:** An entire chapter of *Creative Serging Illustrated* (pages 64-75) is devoted to flatlocking. Refer to it for basic how-to information.

Many of our readers complain about flatlocking that's not flat. (After being flatlocked, the stitches won't pull flat, but instead form a ridge on the right side. See Fig. 4-14.) Whether it's a 2-

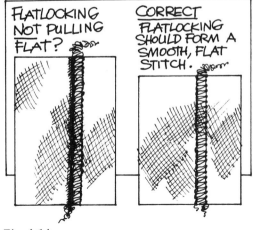

Fig. 4-14

thread or 3-thread flatlock, *the secrets to flatter flatlocking are having a sufficiently loosened needle thread and allowing the stitches to hang over the edge.*

The needle thread of the 2-thread should be loose enough to overlock with the looper thread beyond the edge of the fabric (Fig. 4-15). The needle

2-THREAD FLATLOCK:
LOOSEN NEEDLE THREAD TO INTER-LOCK WITH LOOPER THREAD BEYOND EDGE.

TOPSIDE
LOWER LOOPER THREAD
UNDERSIDE
NEEDLE THREAD

Fig. 4-15

thread of a 3-thread flatlock should be loose enough to overlock with the upper looper thread beyond the edge of the fabric; the lower looper should be tightened considerably, enough to form a straight line on the edge of the fabric (Fig. 4-16).

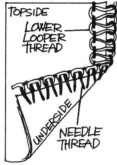

3-THREAD FLATLOCK:
NEEDLE THREAD LOOSENED TO INTERLOCK WITH UPPER LOOPER THREAD BEYOND EDGE. LOWER LOOPER TIGHTENED TO A STRAIGHT LINE.

TOPSIDE
UPPER LOOPER THREAD
LOWER LOOPER THREAD
UNDERSIDE
NEEDLE THREAD

Fig. 4-16

When flatlocking (either 2- or 3-thread), *allow the flatlock stitches to hang over the edges or fold of the fabric half the width of the stitch.* (Pretrim seams, if necessary, because you will not be trimming any fabric while flatlocking.) Then, when the stitch is pulled flat, there will be room for the fabric to lie flat under the stitches. See Fig. 4-17.

KEY TO FLAT FLATLOCKING: ALLOW STITCHES TO HANG OVER EDGE.

Fig. 4-17   FABRIC FOLD

5. *Serged Embellishments*

Because of the looper threads, any overlock stitch has embellishment potential. Even when the serger is using regular thread, the loopers form an intricate design infinitely variable with stitch width, stitch length, and tension adjustments. Add the element of decorative thread in or under the overlock stitch, and the embellishment becomes more dramatic.

Invisible (Well, Almost) Embellishment Secrets

Fine, monofilament nylon can be the key to serged embellishment success; the thread secures discreetly, directing the focus to the other stitch elements, colors, and textures. Now that a softer, more subtle size (#80 or .004 mm) is readily available to home sewers, you'll discover a multitude of applications:

• **Floating decorative flatlocking.** Use monofilament nylon in the needle of 2-thread flatlocking or the needle and lower looper of 3-thread flatlocking. Decorative thread used in the looper or upper looper looks as if it is floating on the fabric surface.

• **Sequin, pearl, or bead strand applications** (see page 63). Use monofilament nylon in the needle and looper(s); the thread will disappear, allowing the strand to float along the edge.

• **Rolled edge hemming on any hard-to-match fabric.** Works wonderfully on metallics and laces. Finer (#80) invisible threads will produce softer rolled edges; for stiffer rolled edges, use heavier monofilament or fishing line techniques (see page 60).

Narrow Rolled Hem Edge

☞ **Update tip:** Because #80 monofilament nylon is so fine, it is not recommended for serged seaming. Other heavier, stronger monofilament thread (#60) can be used. Also, Janet Stocker of Treadleart warns that nylon thread is heat-sensitive; avoid contact with irons on hot settings. (Fortunately, their press testing failed to melt *Wonder Thread*, the nylon thread she sells.)

Sources: Contact suppliers such as
Aardvark Adventures *(Nylon Filament)*,
Clotilde *(Invisible Nylon Thread)*,
Nancy's Notions *(Monofilament Nylon
Thread)*, Speed Stitch *(Nylon Filament)*,
Treadleart *(Wonder Thread)*, and YLI
(Miracle Nylon) (for addresses, see
"Serge-by-Mail-Directory," pages 163-
173). Be sure to specify size; #80 is
finer than #60.

Serged Piping

In a seam or on an edge, piping out-
lines and strengthens. Because selections of packaged pipings are limited,
seamsters often create custom versions
using conventional sewing machines.
Now sergers also offer piping-making
potential. Not only are serged pipings
less expensive than their straight-sewn
counterparts (no extra fabric to buy for
bias strips), they are also faster to make
(no cutting or piecing).

Making Your Own Piping

• Buy a roll of 1 1/4"-wide *Seams
Great®*, the foundation strip (bias
tricot) for serged piping. (Forget the
time-consuming task of cutting your
own.)

• Gather lots of ingredients—enough
for the piping, testing, and reject
segments. First, measure the seam
and/or edge to be piped. *You'll need
ten times that length* of any decorative
thread or filler cord; use the excess for
testing. A clear, fine monofilament
thread is used for the invisible serging
integral to most of the piping techniques; have at least one spool or cone
on hand of size #80, or, if not, the
slightly heavier size #60.

• Use filler cord (like pearl cotton) on
cones (not balls) for smoothest, most
carefree feeding; lay in your lap or on
the floor.

• *Place the filler cord, cording, or bead
trim under the back of the foot and over the
front of the foot, between the needle and
knife.* Butt the cord, cording, or bead

trim up against, and just to the left of, the foot front ledge, as shown in Fig. 5-1.

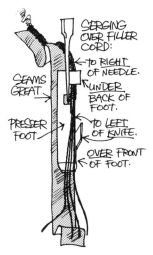

Fig. 5-1

For some models, you may need to remove the presser foot (see page 58, Fig. 5-10). Start serging (holding the threads taut); if you like the results, slip the bias strip under the foot, next to the feed dogs. As you serge, trim off about 1/2" of the tricot, being careful not to stretch this strip or cut what's being applied.

☞ **Update tip:** *Creative Serging Illustrated* shows folding the bias strip over the filler cord, then serging along the fold. Serging with the filler cord on top, as described above, is easier.

• **Serge slowly.**

• If your serger has a cording foot, slot, or groove, insert the filler cord, cordings, or trim if their diameter is narrow enough to fit through or under.

• If the finished piping seems too heavy, decrease the number of filler-cord strands, or, if using decorative thread or yarn, lengthen the stitch.

• **To create twisted pearl cotton cording,** secure four strands (at least twice the length needed) to a hole in an empty bobbin. Place on your conventional machine's bobbin winder; wind until the degree of twist desired is even throughout. After winding, grasp the twisted strands at the halfway point; the *cord will automatically twist around itself, doubling its thickness.* Straighten any curlicues by pulling on the cord lengthwise. The twisting can also be done by hand (secure one end, attach the other end to a pencil, and twist), although your bobbin winder is faster. See Fig. 5-2.

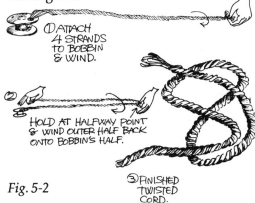

Fig. 5-2

• Serge plenty of piping so that you can cut away imperfect sections and save the best for applications. After enough piping has been made, lift the presser foot, place the filler to the left of the foot, and slowly serge off the piping edge.

Types of Serged Piping

Filler-cord piping. Adjust for a satin (short) rolled-edge stitch and serge over three to four strands of pearl cotton. Adjust tensions for the rolled edge to achieve the thread coverage desired (loosen the upper looper,

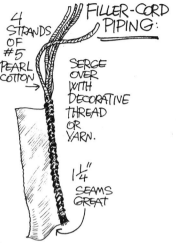

Fig. 5-3

tighten the lower looper). See Fig. 5-3. Thread or yarn recommended for the upper looper: woolly stretch nylon, fine metallic knitting yarn (*YLI's Candlelight*), pearl cotton, rayon topstitching thread (*YLI's Pearl Crown Rayon*), and braided rayon ribbon (*Ribbon Thread* or *Ribbon Floss*).

Pearl cotton piping. This version differs from the filler-cord piping because the pearl cotton shows. Adjust for a medium-length rolled edge and serge over strands of pearl cotton (four for 1/8" width, eight for 1/4" width). Use monofilament nylon thread in the upper looper. You'll love the look of the twisted variation, applied in the same manner as the untwisted strands (see Fig. 5-4).

Fig. 5-4

Purchased cord or braid piping. Adjust for a long, wide balanced stitch, and serge over the cord or braid. Use monofilament nylon thread in the upper looper. When applying thick cord, you may need to remove the presser foot; hold the cord taut, guiding it between the needle (on the left) and the knife (on the right). Gradually tighten the lower looper so that no loops stick out beyond the cord edge. See Fig. 5-5.

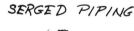

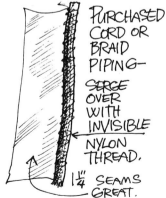

Fig. 5-5

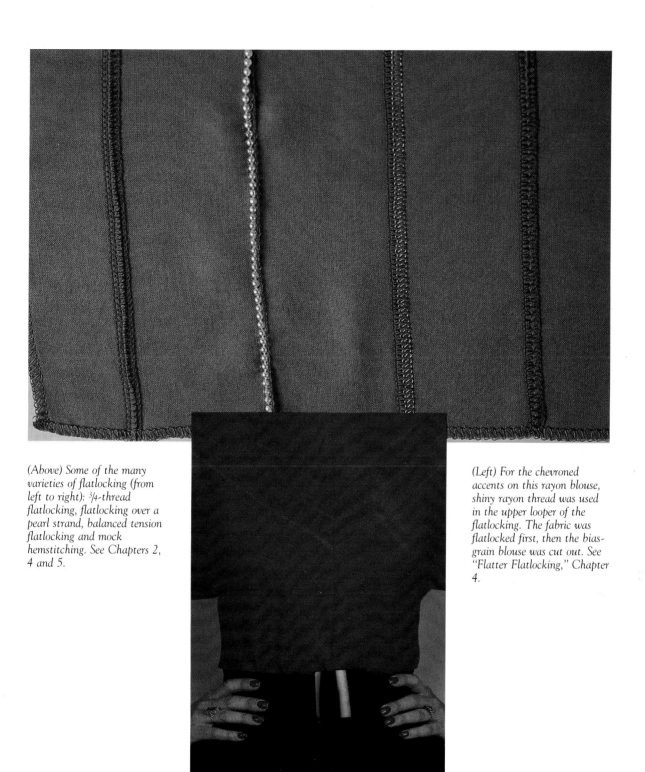

(Above) Some of the many varieties of flatlocking (from left to right): ³/4-thread flatlocking, flatlocking over a pearl strand, balanced tension flatlocking and mock hemstitching. See Chapters 2, 4 and 5.

(Left) For the chevroned accents on this rayon blouse, shiny rayon thread was used in the upper looper of the flatlocking. The fabric was flatlocked first, then the bias-grain blouse was cut out. See "Flatter Flatlocking," Chapter 4.

(Above) Using any of these serge-turn-and-topstitch techniques and edge-finishing is fast, lightweight and facingless. See "Modular Knit Know-How," Chapter 2.

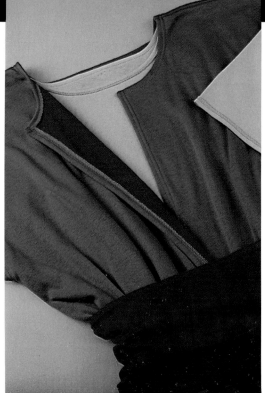

(Left) For this reversible top, the turquoise and hot pink knits were placed wrong sides together and edge finished as one layer. See Chapter 2.

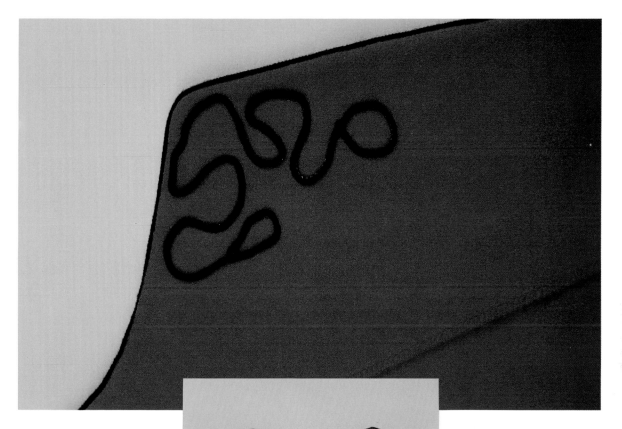

(Above) Because melt adhesive thread was used in the lower looper, the serged cord could be easily pressed into the scrolled motifs. See "Serged Scrollwork: Couching," Chapter 5.

(Left) Serged piping coordinates exactly with the serged scrollwork on this unlined wool jacket; cotton crochet thread (in the upper looper) was used to make both the piping and scrollwork cord. See "Serged Piping," Chapter 5.

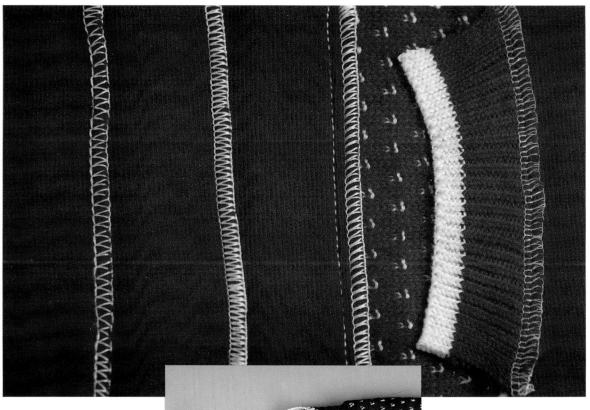

(Above) Sweater seams, from left to right: 1-a stretched-out problem, 2-differential feeding solves the stretching problem, 3-straight stitching and then serge-finishing also controls stretching, and 4-ribbing serge-seamed in the relaxed position to eliminate waving. See Chapter 6.

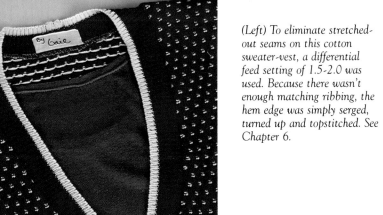

(Left) To eliminate stretched-out seams on this cotton sweater-vest, a differential feed setting of 1.5-2.0 was used. Because there wasn't enough matching ribbing, the hem edge was simply serged, turned up and topstitched. See Chapter 6.

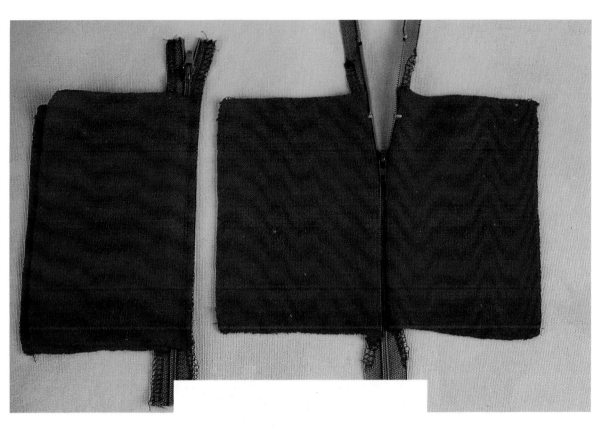

(Above) Using a zipper at least 4" longer than the opening (let 2" extend beyond each end), serge, trimming the tape about 1/8". Bartack the ends to secure the pull and teeth. See Chapter 1.

(Left) A serged zipper application was used in the ribbed collar of this wool doubleknit top. After the zipper was serged into the collar, it was faced with the contrasting ribbing. See Chapter 1.

On this speed-tailored jacket, the lining was serge-seamed (except for the sleeves, which were set-in with straight stitching and then serge-finished), and the exposed edge of the facing was neatly serge-finished. See Chapter 3.

(Above) To minimize bulk, the neckline of this silk blouse was faced and serged-finished, wrong sides together. The sequin trim was quickly hand tacked in place. See Chapter 7.

(Left) Because this dressy blouse is fitted, seams were serge-finished first, then straight stitched and pressed open. See Chapters 7 and 10.

The patchworked inset on this placemat was serge-pieced; the border was serge-finished with durable all-purpose thread. For extra body and color interest, the napkins were made double layer and serge-finished together with woolly stretch nylon. See "Never-Miss Mitered Placemats," Chapter 11.

PURCHASED CORD PIPING/
WOOL TWEED.

Bead trim piping. (Using glass bead or pearl strand trim, see pages 63-64.) Adjust for a medium-length rolled edge. Thread the upper looper with monofilament thread. Remove the presser foot. See Fig. 5-6.

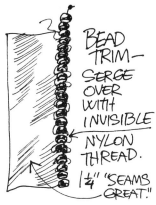

BEAD TRIM— SERGE OVER WITH INVISIBLE NYLON THREAD. 1¼" "SEAMS GREAT."

Fig. 5-6

Update tip: A bead trim application foot is now available for the Pfaff Hobbylocks (see page 141). Several other serger companies are developing a similar bead or pearl trim application foot. Check with your dealer.

Applying the Piping

Note: Preshrink piping that is susceptible to shrinking. Wash and dry as you will the finished project. Place in a lingerie bag to prevent tangling. Press to straighten.

Either apply the piping with conventional straight-stitching and a zipper foot, as shown in Fig. 5-7, or use a piping application foot for sergers. As its name implies, the piping foot guarantees smooth serging of piped seams and edges because it has a groove in the underside (see page 140).

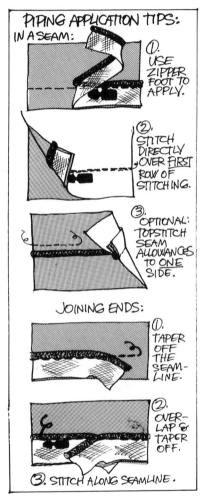

Fig. 5-7

With a conventional machine and a zipper foot, straight-stitch the piping to the seamline, right sides together, as shown in Step 1 of Fig. 5-7. Use a long stitch (6-8 stitches per inch). Then, sandwich the piping between the seam, right sides together, as shown. *(The straight-stitching should be on top, as a guide for the serging.)*

With a 3- or 3/4-thread overlock stitch, serge-seam, aligning the piping line in the foot groove. See Fig. 5-8.

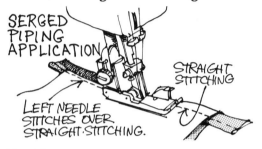

Fig. 5-8

(Without a piping foot, you will need to hold the fabric layers securely in front of and behin the foot to ensure straight-stitching over the piping line). *The left serger needle should stitch directly over the straight-stitching.* To control bulk, press the seam allowances away from the piping; edge-stitching is optional.

☞ **Update tip:** If you own an ElnaLock L-1, L-2, L-5, or PRO-4, the optional Tape Guide attachment (see page 141) forms piping automatically. (Ask your dealer for a demonstration.)

Sources: For decorative thread suppliers, turn to "Serge-by-Mail Directory," (look under Great Serger Notions, page 166).

Serged Scrollwork: Couching

Spiegel, Honey Bee, and Lew Magram catalogs describe it as "soutache braid" (even if it's not made of soutache braid) or "passementerie" (pas-men-tree). The technique may be more familiar to you as "couching," the traditional name for this enticing embellishment, a narrow, flexible braid, yarn, or cording that is sewn in a looped pattern to decorate fashions or furnishings. Your serger can expand the couching possibilities far beyond the limits of soutache braid.

Study ready-to-wear examples in stores and catalogs. Typically, a simple garment is the foundation for the couching, which accents a confined area—a yoke, lapel, wide waistband, placket, or corner of a shawl. (*Overdoing it can transform fashion into costume. If you're couching-crazy, do it on pillows.*) Favorite schemes are worked on lush, beefy knits and tweeds; sewing burrows the braid into the spongy fabric surface. Boiled wool (see page 36) is perfect.

Eliminate very heavy, ribbed, or textured fabrics that would be a hassle to mark and couch. As for color, generally the couched braid contrasts with the foundation fabric, but don't rule out tone-on-tone for subtle elegance.

Types of Couching

If you're creating serged braid to be couched on a sewing machine, the scrolled patterns can be more sharply curved, intricate, and concentrated. The conventionally applied method will be outlined below, but here are other alternatives that utilize serging:

• **Serged couching,** which is flatlocking over a braid, cord, or yarn, must necessarily be straighter, offering the options of loops (Fig. 5-9). Remember,

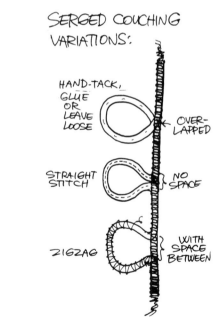

Fig. 5-9

because of the horizontal looper action, the embellishment must be couched along an edge or fold (Fig. 5-10). Also

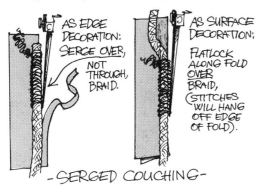

AS EDGE DECORATION: SERGE OVER, NOT THROUGH, BRAID.

AS SURFACE DECORATION: FLATLOCK ALONG FOLD OVER BRAID, (STITCHES WILL HANG OFF EDGE OF FOLD).

— SERGED COUCHING —

Fig. 5-10

see page 69 of *Creative Serging Illustrated.*

Ervena Yu, author of the *Stylish Serging* series, which includes volumes *I, II, III,* and *IV* (see "References," page 174), is famous for her free-form looping techniques. On one couched garment in *Stylish Serging I,* a bead was hung on the braid loop before continuing to serge down the next section of braid. On another, a bead strand was couched randomly, allowing intermittent lengths to drape freely.

COUCHED BEADING APPLICATION IN ABSTRACT DESIGN.

FROM: STYLISH SERGING I.

FROM: STYLISH SERGING III

FLAT-LOCKED PLAID

• **Faux couching** is simulating the look of the applied braid with decorative-thread serging along an edge or flat-locked on the surface. Updated versions of couching can be created with the straight lines applied in argyle and plaid arrangements. See Fig. 5-11.

— FAUX COUCHING —

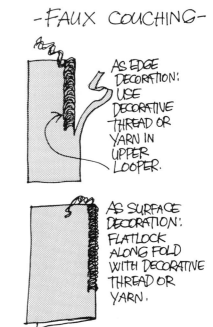

AS EDGE DECORATION: USE DECORATIVE THREAD OR YARN IN UPPER LOOPER.

AS SURFACE DECORATION: FLATLOCK ALONG FOLD WITH DECORATIVE THREAD OR YARN.

Fig. 5-11

Creating Serged Braid for Conventional Couching

When creating braid to be couched conventionally on a sewing machine, *the firmer the decorative ribbon, thread, or yarn used in the upper looper, the better.* You will not be serging on fabric here—Robbie calls it "serging on air." The threads themselves create the braid.

• Adjust for short, rolled edge serging. To avoid jamming, begin by serging over cloth (for 2-3"), then chain off, holding the stitches slightly taut. Vary the upper looper tension and stitch length until you achieve the look desired. See Fig. 5-12. Gail loved the braid made from Wright's *Flexi-braid;* it was used in the upper looper, with all-purpose thread in the needle and lower looper.

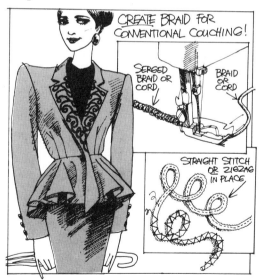

Fig. 5-12

☞ **Update tip:** Using the same color thread throughout will make the braid more reversible and less tricky to apply uniformly. Other upper looper threads we recommend are: *Ribbon Thread* or *Ribbon Floss* and six-strand embroidery thread (see page 41).

• Approximate the amount of braid required, and take a few moments to serge two yards more for testing.

Couching the Serged Braid

1. Since flat pieces are easier to mark and couch, **sew as few seams in the project as possible.** If using fusible interfacing, fuse in place before marking or couching.

2. **Transfer the couching design to the fabric.** The design can be drawn freehand or traced from a Battenberg lace outline. (You can buy Battenberg lace patterns at most fabric and needlework stores.) For transferring the scrolling, try the *Iron-On Transfer Pencil*, sold in notions departments and in the Clotilde, Nancy's Notions, and Serge & Sew Notions catalogs (see "Serge-by-Mail Directory," pages 163-173). Following the package how-to's, draw or trace on paper and press the paper onto the fabric. For dark fabrics, try light tracing paper or tailor's chalk. The transfer will be a mirror image.

3. **Make a test on scrap fabric:** Lay the braid on the scroll lines, pinning or glue-sticking to secure temporarily. *If the serged braid is conspicuously two-sided, be careful to manipulate the same side up throughout.*

4. With a long zigzag (wide enough to cover the braid), **stitch the braid in place;** for invisible stitching, use fine monofilament thread. Because serged braids are inherently flatter than purchased braids, you shouldn't have problems with even stitching using a standard foot. However, if your stitches tend to fall off the braid, either zigzag with a slotted cording foot, remove the presser foot (it should still be lowered) and free-machine embroider, or stitch alongside with an adjustable zipper foot. The braid can also be straight-stitched or couched with a blind-hem stitch; a twin needle works well for wider braids. See Fig. 5-12.

Flash! **Couching braid update:** Right before sending this book to the printer, we made braid with *Threadfuse™* melt adhesive thread (see page 40) as the lower looper thread. The lower looper was not tightened all the way down, so that more of the melt adhesive combithread was exposed. *Because of the thread's fusible component, the braid made using it can easily be shaped and fused to the couching outline.* All you do is shape the braid, pinning intermittently; steam baste; remove the pins; and finally press, protecting with a press cloth (Fig. 5-13). The couching stitch-

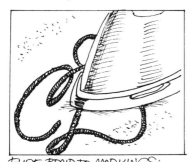

FUSE BRAID TO MARKINGS.

Fig. 5-13

ing is smoother, too, because the braid is secure without pinning (Fig. 5-14).

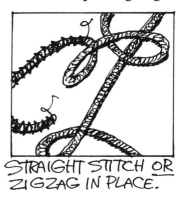

STRAIGHT STITCH OR ZIGZAG IN PLACE.

Fig. 5-14

Fishing Line Flounces

Fishing line flounces? If you're wondering what fishing has to do with flouncing, browse through a bridal/formal wear shop or department. Flounced ruffles, abundant on so many styles this season, now stand out in fluted fashion. The reason? Fishing line has been serged into the ruffle edge to create extra body and to enhance flouncing. It's easy to master the technique.

✎ **Note:** Read through the steps given on pages 61-62 first. Then test this technique on fabric scraps before serging the garment ruffles. To alter the look, vary the fishing line weight, thread type, stitch length, degree of stretching, fabric weight, or grain.

Choose your pattern and fabric.
The garments are usually dressy, like this tiered prom dress and elegantly ruffled blouse. Of course, the method is perfect for wedding party ruffles, from the flower girl's frills to the bride's gown and veil.

Our testing shows that a wide range of fabrics, from sheers to medium weights, can be used—tulle, chiffon, broadcloth, crepe, lace, satin, jersey. In fact, the fabric weight didn't alter the ruffling as much as the weight of the fishing line. Finer line produced a more ruffled, curled edge; heavier line resulted in a more flared edge.

☞ **Update tip:** If it's costume-making season again, why not take advantage of fishing line flouncing and inexpensive, wide-width tulle? Tulle costs as little as $.89/yard and is available in several shades.

Shop for the fishing line. You'll find it at most drug, discount, and sporting goods stores. Remember, the heavier the pound weight of the line, the coarser it is. (Evidently this corresponds to the weight of the fish being pursued.) Keep your selection within the 12- to 40-pound range. One bridal specialist consulted prefers 25-pound line; another more frequently serges in 12-pound" test." Buy shorter yardages first, test, and then determine which weight produces the desired look for a particular project. Prices and put-ups for the fishing line generally run as follows:

- 12-pound line—500 yards, $4.69; 20 yards, $.89

- 25-pound line—250 yards, $1.59; 20 yards, $.89

- 40-pound line—100 yards, $1.39 (usually not available in shorter yardages)

Once you have your materials, **you're ready to follow these steps:**

1. **Cut the ruffle strips.** Allow 1/4" to 3/8" for trimming on the serged edge. Bias grain will yield the most curl at the ruffle edge (and arguably the prettiest ruffle), but the crosswise grain of some fabrics, particularly jersey knits, will also make lush ruffles. Limit the use of lengthwise grain ruffles to "no-grain" fabrics like tulle and netting.

2. **Adjust your serger for narrow rolled or balanced edge hemming** (test to see which you prefer). Use a short- to medium-length stitch, whichever covers the raw edge and fishing line adequately.

3. Get ready to serge. In addition to fishing line as long as the ruffle, **allow a very long tail at the end, about half the ruffle length.** When starting, serge over the line for 2"-3". For easiest handling, *serge with the fishing line going over the front of the foot (just to the right of the needle and the left of the knife) and under the back of the foot.* If the serger foot has a right-hand front ledge, butt the fishing line against the left side of the foot ledge so that it will be automatically guided, cut-free, between the needle and the knife (Fig. 5-15). Or, if

you have a cording foot, simply feed the line through the hole. Trim off about 1/8" of the ruffle edge while serge finishing. **DO NOT STRETCH THE EDGE AS YOU SERGE.**

☞ **Update tip:** Some how-to's recommend rolling the edge over the line (which means placing the line under the fabric), but guiding the fishing line accurately from this position is tricky at best. Stick with the method described above.

4. **Serge off the end of the ruffle,** *le*aving a tail of line about half the ruffle length. Pull the fishing line tail to the left, away from the knife, to prevent cutting.

5. **Stretch the serged edge to create the flouncing.** The stretching and resultant flouncing will shorten the excess fishing line tails. Trim the fishing line to the serging, securing with seam sealant.

☞ **Update tip:** To gather the raw edge of lightweight ruffles, adjust for balanced, wide, long serging. Tighten the needle tension to serge and gather simultaneously. Or, if your serger has the differential feed feature, set on the "2" setting to gather. For heavier fabrics, serge with the wide, long stitch over a strand of fishing line; then, secure one end and pull up the other to gather.

NARROW ROLLED EDGE.

Fig. 5-15

Serging Bead Strands

Incredibly, three-dimensional bead, sequin, or pearl strands can be applied with your serger. Follow the steps outlined below to achieve an elegantly edged finish.

SERGER APPLIED PEARL TRIM.

Attaching with a rolled edge:

1. Adjust your serger for narrow rolled hemming (consult your owner's manual, if necessary). **Select a stitch length just longer than an individual bead diameter.** If possible, adjust the bite (the distance between the needle and the knife) to be slightly wider than normal.

☞ **Update tips:** *Buy the tiniest beading available.* Also, depending on the serger make and model, a regular standard width overlock stitch may work better than a narrow rolled hem. Test.

For inconspicuous serging, use fine monofilament nylon (for details, see pages 41 and 51).

If you have a special beading applicator foot (see page 141), serge as usual, allowing the strand to feed through the slot, automatically guided between the needle and the knife. Ask your dealer if there's a similar foot to fit your machine. If not, proceed with this step.

2. *Insert one end of the bead strand under the back of the presser foot and over the front of the foot, riding between the needle and the knives. (Butt the strand against the left side of the front foot ledge.)* Lower the foot and stitch, keeping the bead strand taut as it passes under the foot; this will prevent puckering. See Fig. 5-16.

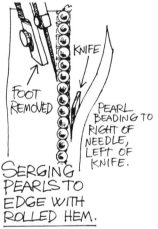

SERGING PEARLS TO EDGE WITH ROLLED HEM.

Fig. 5-16

☞ **Update tip:** Some serger presser feet do not allow enough clearance behind the needle for the bead strand to fit underneath. If you encounter this problem, remove the foot entirely (as shown in Fig. 5-16) and guide the fabric and beads through manually. Again, the strand should be held taut and carefully aligned between the needle on the left and the knives on the right. Also, in Nancy Zieman's videotape, *Sewing for the Bride*, this well-known expert recommends NOT lowering the presser foot; she keeps it in the raised position while serging the strand.

3. **Serge slowly,** guiding the fabric and beading. If you have removed the foot, gently pull the fabric from the back.

Attaching with flatlocking:

1. **Adjust for flatlocking** (see Chapter 8 of *Creative Serging Illustrated*). The stitch width should be about that of an individual bead's diameter. The stitch length should be just longer than the bead's diameter.

2. Fold the fabric and place under the foot. Anchor with the needle.

3. Position the bead strand as described in "Attaching with a Rolled Edge," Step 2, above. *The stitch should hang over the edge of the fold, as shown, so that the fold will flatten after being flat-locked. See Fig. 5-17.*

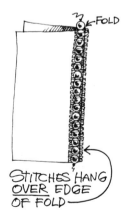

Fig. 5-17

4. **Pull the stitch flat** (Fig. 5-18). It should look as if the bead strand is floating on the fabric. By hand, arrange any visible threads between the beads.

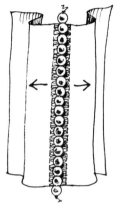

Fig. 5-18

Serged Appliqués

Sewing pro Andrea Nynas (of the Viking Sewing Machine Company) devised this innovative appliqué technique: three-dimensional appliqué.

Suggested appliqué ideas: Leaves on a tree, feathers on a bird, petals on flowers. Several serged appliqué design and project inspirations are featured in *Distinctive Serger Gifts and Crafts, An Idea Book for All Occasions* (see page 174).

1. First, cut out, then serge-finish with a rolled edge around each appliqué shape—*curves should be gentle.* (Thread tails can be secured with seam sealant or hidden under stitched-down sections of the appliqué.)

2. Position the serged fabric pieces in place on the background as in traditional appliqué. Then use your conventional sewing machine to straight-stitch the fabric pieces in place (stitching right next to the inner rolled edge on each fabric shape). *Don't stitch completely around each appliqué;* leave some areas unstitched so that they are not flat, creating a three-dimensional effect. See Fig. 5-19.

Fig. 5-19

☞ **Update tip:** The serge-finished appliqués can also be applied flat. After arranging the appliqué design, straight-stitch completely around each shape. Author Ervena Yu often selects Ultrasuede® for her appliqués; the

nonwoven synthetic suede holds the stitch width consistently, producing a beautifully uniform, clean edge finish. (When using heavier fabrics like Ultrasuede®, serge-finish with a wider, balanced stitch.)

Serger Cutwork?

Whenever serger cutwork is introduced to a class, dubious students ask, *"Isn't it just easier to use a regular sewing*

machine?" The answer is, "Yes, sometimes." But as long as you follow a few ground rules, serging cutwork is a fascinating, easy-to-master embellishment, more supple than its satin-stitched cousin.

Prerequisites for serging cutwork include:

• **A serger that has a removable presser foot.** (Therefore, the stitch finger cannot be on the presser foot.)

• **Narrow rolled or balanced edge stitching capability,** either 2-thread or 3-thread.

• **Gently curved, not-too-intricate cutwork design.**

• **Tightly constructed, blouse-weight, or lighter fabric.** Unlike conventional machine cutwork (which can be stitched on coarser fabric), serger cutwork success is dependent on firmly woven fabric no heavier than broadcloth. Batiste is a favorite. Remember, you will be reinforcing the design area with lightweight fusible interfacing.

• **Fine thread.** Lingerie or machine embroidery types are the most trouble-free and produce the most delicate edge. Rayon thread is lovely, but can be prone to breaking and stitching unevenly. For your first project, choose a color that matches the project; inconsistencies in stitch quality will be less apparent.

• **Patience and practice.** Don't expect to master serger cutwork in minutes. Always test using the same thread, stitch settings, cutwork shapes, interfacing, and fabric.

Now you're ready for an exciting adventure in creativity. Start with small projects—handkerchiefs, removable collars, scarves. Or, accent an area of a garment—yokes, collars, cuffs, pockets. Look for styles that are simple, with minimal seaming and other dressmaker details; the cutwork should be the design focal point.

Stencil patterns and Battenberg lace designs are both good sources for cutwork shapes. Stick with simple motifs and with shapes having few angles and sharp points. Sergeable shapes include rounded teardrops, diamonds, and leaves, because stitching will be continuous. If in doubt, serge the prospective cutout on a scrap of the actual project fabric.

☞ **Update tip:** Stitch the cutwork on the fabric first, then position the pattern and cut out the garment. This method will ensure proper placement of the cutwork on larger garment sections like bodices.

1. **Transfer the cutwork design** onto the right side (nonadhesive side) of lightweight fusible nonwoven interfacing. (Use water-soluble markers sparingly.) Fuse lightweight interfacing to the wrong side of the cutwork area.

2. **Straight-stitch to outline the cutwork design.** Sew from the interfacing side with a short stitch length (about 20/inch) and thread that matches the

fabric. This stitching serves to stabilize the cutwork edges as well as transfer the motif. See Fig. 5-20.

Fig. 5-20

3. With sharp, small scissors, **trim to the straight-stitching one area at a time.** Alternate between trimming and serge-finishing (next steps).

4. Adjust the serger settings and thread for cutwork finishing. Use fine thread in the needle and looper(s). **Set up your serger for narrow rolled or balanced edge serging.** For durability, 2-thread serging should be rolled. Stitch length should be the shortest possible. Finally, remove the presser foot and disengage the upper knife. If you can't disengage the knife, be careful not to cut your project while serge finishing the cutwork. Adjust tensions while test-serging on the actual project fabric.

5. To best manipulate the fabric, *fold the cutwork cutout in half, right sides together*, as shown in Fig. 5-21. **Start**

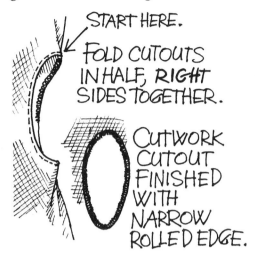

Fig. 5-21

serging on a single thickness, gently pulling the edge under the needle. Maintain an even, SLOW speed. Continue to refold the cutout to serge through a single thickness of the edge. After completing the edge finishing, overlap the stitches slightly and chain off. Secure the thread ends with a drop of seam sealant, allow to dry, and clip the tails.

6. Repeat Steps 3-5 until the motif is completed.

☞ **Update tip:** Fill in larger cutwork with laces or sheers—pin in place and straight-stitch close to the serging through all layers. Trim away any excess fabric. Or, embellish the cutwork borders with decorative machine embroidery stitches worked on your conventional machine.

6. Update: The Latest on Serging Sweaters

Gail has continued to test-serge sweaterknits since writing "Sensational Serged Sweaters" for *Creative Serging Illustrated*. Her newest findings, compiled for this chapter, will help guarantee sweater-making success, even if you're a first-timer.

Secrets for Serging Cotton and Other Stretchy Sweaterknits

Ah, cotton sweatering. Somehow, its many virtues—*incredible comfort in any climate, washability, color depth, packability*—outweigh its drawbacks of stretching out, shrinkage, and fading. Ready-made cotton sweaters can be picked up for as little as $25, but sewing's still the smarter option. How so, you ask? *Because your serged sweater will look, feel, fit, and launder better*; it will be preshrunk to eliminate the shrinkage that plagues all ready-mades. Your custom version will be made and will remain the most flattering length and size. If that's not convincing enough, the time required will be only an hour or two, even if you're a newcomer to cotton sweater sewing.

Plentiful Patterns

Sweater patterns, once scarce, are now found in every pattern company's "Knits and Sportswear Separates" tab section. Actually, any simple knit top pattern will work—avoid darts and extra seams, and for the fastest sewing, skip closures too. Knit specialists like *Kwik-Sew* and *Stretch & Sew* have the largest and most varied style selections. The deep V neckline and sleeveless features of this tunic top are particularly slenderizing and easy to sew from cotton sweatering. Layer this top over a T-shirt and slacks or a dress. When cooler weather calls, wear longer sleeves and higher necklines underneath.

☞ **Update tip:** Because cotton sweatering grows as you wear it, you'll need to "size down"—buy one pattern size smaller than usual. Or you can buy your standard pattern size, but sew with 1" seam allowances; try this approach on your first project, safety pin-fitting the sweaterknit pieces first before seaming.

Another alternative is using hand-knitting blocking diagrams as sweater patterns. Add 1" seam allowances and substitute ribbed bands or ribbing-by-the-yard for those shown knit-in. Some instructions include full-size blocking patterns, which work well as sewing patterns (add seams). But most others must be enlarged or drawn from small-scale measurement guides and transferred to pattern tissue, nonwoven fabric, or butcher paper. (Enlarging is easier than it sounds; most diagrams include only two or three rectangular pieces.) See Fig. 6-1.

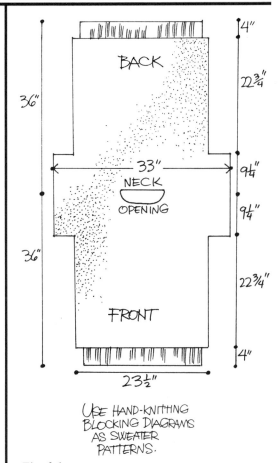

Fig. 6-1

Sweaterknit Fabric Options and Sources

Cotton sweatering is available at your local fabric stores or by mail. Shop before resorting to mail order; these days, the majority of retailers are carrying at least some cotton sweater-knits and ribbings, particularly during warmer months. If inventories in your area are devoid of sweaterings, write the mail-order companies listed on pages 169-170.

Single-knit jerseys, in a variety of weights and stitches, are the most prevalent; these cotton sweaterings tend to stretch out because both the stitch and fiber lack resiliency (Fig. 6-2). *A goof-proof project choice would be a medium-weight sweatering with enough thickness and texture to disguise any less-than-precise sewing.* To bolster stretchability and body, use ribbing-by-the-yard for the entire sweater; finer, 1 knit by 1 purl ribbing (2 knit by 2 purl is shown in Fig. 6-2) is less bulky and can double capably as sweater fabric.

COMMON COTTON SWEATERING

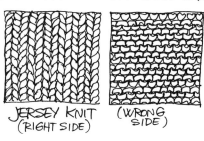

JERSEY KNIT (RIGHT SIDE)

(WRONG SIDE)

RIBBING (RIGHT OR WRONG SIDE.)

Fig. 6-2

By all means, *buy matching ribbing trim if it's available.* When it comes to cottons, you'll have the best luck with more stable ribbing bands (some now even have an elasticized finished edge) or ribbed knit collars (make sure there's sufficient stretch). See Fig. 6-3. However, ribbing-by-the-yard can frequently be your only choice; for best results, read the binding-with-ribbing application tips to follow.

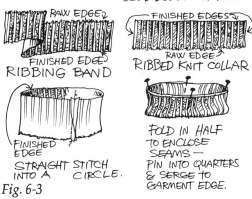

THE MOST STABLE RIBBING: RIBBING BANDS OR RIBBED KNIT COLLARS USED DOUBLE-LAYER.

RAW EDGE
FINISHED EDGE
RIBBING BAND

FINISHED EDGES
RAW EDGE
RIBBED KNIT COLLAR

FINISHED EDGE
STRAIGHT STITCH INTO A CIRCLE.

FOLD IN HALF TO ENCLOSE SEAMS — PIN INTO QUARTERS & SERGE to GARMENT EDGE.

Fig. 6-3

Although many cotton sweaterknits are labeled "needle-ready," they simply aren't. Sweatering labeled as such can shrink as much as 8" per yard. Machine wash and dry the sweatering TWICE before cutting out. Preshrinking compacts the knit structure, making the sweatering easier to handle and richer looking. Ribbing bands, collars, and yardage to be used as trim should NOT be preshrunk; the ribbing becomes difficult to manipulate and apply. (Plus, sweater ribbing that shrinks after sewing provides more edge control.)

☞ **Update tip:** To prevent raveling, serge-finish the edges of sweatering before preshrinking.

Fastest, Most Professional Sweater-Making

• **Rethink seaming strategies—** *remember, most sweater seams should be stable, not stretchy.* The more unstable the cotton sweatering, the more stable the seam should be. Run a few test samples on scraps. Unless there's a differential feed feature at your disposal, sew the seams first on your conventional machine, with a long (8 stitches per inch) stitch and 1" seam allowances. Then, finish with a 2- or 3-thread serged stitch, trimming off the excess allowance and serging the two layers together. See Fig. 6-4.

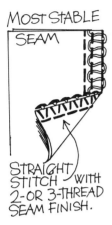

MOST STABLE SEAM

STRAIGHT STITCH WITH 2- OR 3-THREAD SEAM FINISH.

Fig. 6-4

Some sweaterings can be successfully serged in one step; adjust for the widest stitch width and a medium to long stitch and lighten the foot pressure (see your manual for how-to's). Always trim at least 1/2" off, and do not stretch the fabric as you serge. If you can, you should still stick with more stable stitches—a 3/4-thread overlock, a 4/2-thread chainstitch/overedge, or a 5-thread chainstitch/overlock.

If the seam waves, try force-feeding the fabric layers under the foot while holding the layers against the back of the foot. This force-feeding is done automatically with differential feeding—set the dial up to "2" to ease the fabric layers and prevent stretching. Also, lengthen the stitch and continue to lighten the foot pressure.

No matter what seaming method is used on other parts of the sweater, *straight-stitch the shoulders.* Finish the

seam edges with serging, press open, and topstitch 1/4" on both sides of the seamline. These pressed-open seams will be stable and flat, a smooth surface for shoulder pads. See Fig. 6-5.

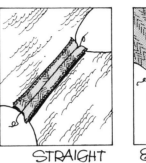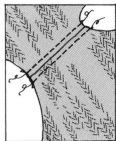

STRAIGHT STITCH A CONVENTIONAL SEAM, PRESS OPEN— & TOPSTITCH.

Fig. 6-5

☞ **Update tip:** Prevent seams mismatching at the bottom edge of rubbed cuffs or side seams by stretching the bottom edge taut (Fig. 6-6).

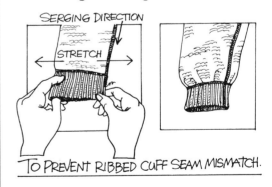

SERGING DIRECTION

STRETCH

TO PREVENT RIBBED CUFF SEAM MISMATCH.

Fig. 6-6

• **Eliminate stretched-out ribbing** by using the more stable ribbing bands or ribbed knit collars double layer (Fig. 6-3). Check the length and stretchability of collars before applying. For example, if you like to push up your sleeves, make sure the wrist ribbing circle will expand to fit your forearm. Also, keep in mind that wider ribbings will be more stable. If you apply ribbing bands single layer, use those at least 1 1/4" wide (finished) to minimize stretching.

For circular applications like crew necklines, bottom edges, and cuffs: sew, fold, quarter, and serge (Fig. 6-3). *Serge with the ribbing on top; the ribbing should be in the relaxed, not the stretched-out, position.* Ease the sweater edge underneath—if you stretch the ribbing while serging it will assume the stretched—out position permanently. See Fig. 6-7. (When the sweater edge is

Fig. 6-7

much wider than the ribbing, easing may not take up the fullness sufficiently; gather the edge to the ribbing before seaming.)

If using less stable ribbing-by-the-yard, bind the edge. An inherent advantage of this binding is that *the neckline or armhole edge will never stretch out.* The stability will rule out using this technique on high necklines, however; a bound edge will not stretch to fit over your head. The finished

binding should be no wider than 1"; cut crosswise ribbing strips three times the finished binding width plus 1/2". Serge-finish one long edge before applying. To apply (Fig. 6-8):

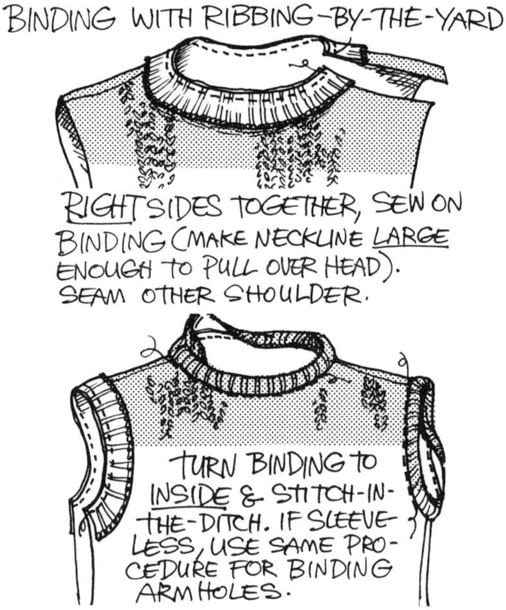

BINDING WITH RIBBING–BY-THE-YARD

RIGHT SIDES TOGETHER, SEW ON BINDING (MAKE NECKLINE LARGE ENOUGH TO PULL OVER HEAD). SEAM OTHER SHOULDER.

TURN BINDING TO INSIDE & STITCH-IN-THE-DITCH. IF SLEEVE-LESS, USE SAME PRO-CEDURE FOR BINDING ARMHOLES.

Fig. 6-8

1. Straight-stitch one shoulder seam and press open.

2. Right sides together, straight-stitch the binding to the edge. The seam allowance will be the width of the finished trim. *Stretch slightly around curves so that the binding will lie flat.* If binding a neckline, try the bound edge over your head, pinning the other shoulder seam (it should be large enough to pull easily on and off).

3. Straight-stitch the other opening seam, *through the binding,* and press open. Trim the shoulder seam bulk.

4. Turn the serge-finished edge of the binding to the inside (the binding should be an even width throughout).

5. Stitch-in-the-ditch to secure the binding in place.

✎ **Note:** For flatter, less bulky bottom hems, simply serge-finish the edge (don't stretch it out), turn up, and twin-needle topstitch.

Twin Needle Topstitching

Guaranteed: Your cotton sweater will grow, even after worn only once. Never fear—you've preshrunk the fabric. Just throw it in the washing machine and dryer and it will instantly shape up. Put it on, warm, right out of the dryer...delicious comfort.

Sources: If unable to locate sweaterings in your local fabric stores, contact ABC Knits, Artknits by Clifford, Marianne's Textile Products (formerly Diversified Products), Golden Needles, Serge and Sew Notions, Sew What's New, Stretch & Sew Fabrics, or The Thrifty Needle. (For addresses, see "Serge-by-Mail Directory," pages 169-170).

Speedy Knit-and-Serged Sweaters

Many serger enthusiasts are stymied by their inability to copy hand-knit sweaters. They can't knit or even if they can knit, the hours required are impossible to find in an already hectic schedule. The answer could be **keyplate knitting.**

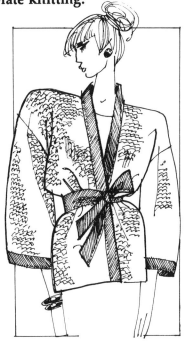

Keyplate knitting is done on a simple, portable frame that has a bed of latch-type needles driven by interchangeable keyplates that determine the stitch size. At an inch-a-minute pace, the production is fast, yet it closely resembles painstaking hand-knit stitches. Hard-to-find specialty supplies are unnecessary; virtually any hand-knitting yarn can be used directly from the skein. Space needed is minimal; setup is easy on any flat surface. Priced at around $250, a keyplate knitter is an affordable equipment addition.

✎ **Note:** Many serger dealers and fabric stores also carry knitting frames, some of which are distributed by the same sewing machine companies that sell sergers. Brand names you'll see are *Baby Knit, Bond, Knit King,* and *Singer,* among others. Watch a demonstration soon; you'll be inspired by the ease and speed of the frame-knitting process.

Even if you've never knitted before, you can quickly master the keyplate technology. Once you do, there are several ways of using the sweaterknit produced. One way is to knit yardage, then cut out the garment and serge the pieces together. An alternative approach is to shape or "full fashion" the pieces as you knit, duplicating the dimensions of simple sewing pattern pieces. Then you can serge to assemble the sweater. Here's how:

1. **Pick the right pattern.** Because of this exciting new angle on knitting, you no longer are limited to using knitting directions for sweaters. Just peruse the nearest sewing pattern catalog (straight garment lines and geometric shapes are the easiest to knit). Refer to Fig. 6-10. Study the pattern piece diagrams on the back of the envelope or on the guidesheet before purchasing. (Our editor, Robbie Fanning, said that in order to look at a pattern's contents, most stores in her area insist you buy it first. However, all the stores we shop in permit the studying of patterns not yet purchased. Ask. Our hunch is that with an explanation, most retailers will be flexible.)

2. **Decide on a yarn.** Remember, it's easier to match fabrics to yarns, than yarns to fabrics. So, when combining sweaterknits and fabrics, select the yarn first. Because the knitting won't be cut, disregard warnings about avoiding ravel-prone shiny or slippery yarns. Any yarn goes, even metallics, mohairs, and slubs.

☞ **Update tip:** Considering a yarn that's color-mixed or ombréd? Buy one sample skein and knit a test swatch; when knit, the color patterning can look completely different than it does on the skein.

3. **Determine the yarn gauge.** Gauge is the number of stitches and rows per square inch, which is essential to calculating the pattern shaping. Knit an entire skein into a rectangle about 70 stitches wide. Allow the swatch to rest overnight, or launder it if you will be washing the finished sweater. Then, measure a 4" square, as shown in Fig. 6-9. Count the number of stitches

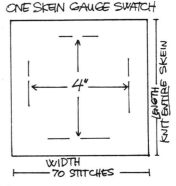

Fig. 6-9

(horizontal) and rows (vertical) in the square. Divide both the stitch and row totals by 4 to calculate the number per inch; the resulting numbers are called the stitch gauge and row gauge.

4. **Calculate the number of rows and stitches required** to shape the pattern pieces. First adapt the pattern by trimming the hems off, trimming seam allowances to 1/4", and straightening curves (Fig. 6-10). (The sweaterknit

Fig. 6-10

will contour to the body without seam curves.) Measure the modified patterns and multiply the crosswise measurements by the stitch gauge (3-1/2 stitches per inch). Multiply the lengthwise measurements by the row gauge (6 rows per inch). To shape the pattern, calculate decreases (periodic reductions in the number of stitches), as shown in Fig. 6-11.

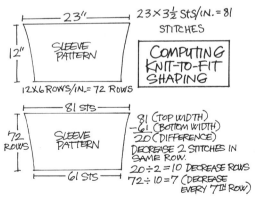

Fig. 6-11

5. Now the math is over and the knitting begins. **Knit each piece,**

making mirror images for fronts, backs, and other seamed sections. Block each knitted piece; use the pattern tissues as blocking guides. Pin to an ironing board or padded surface and steam generously, without touching the iron to the knit. Allow to cool and dry completely.

6. **Serge to assemble.** Consult "Secrets for Serging Cotton and Other Stretchy Sweaterknits," pages 70-71, for seaming solutions. (Unlike cut-and-sewn sweaters, the crosswise edges will be stabilized by the bind-off row. Also, because the edges are finished and more stable, trimming while serge-seaming isn't essential.)

7. **Finish the front edges** with fabric bands or binding. To offset the weight difference between the fabric and sweaterknit, interface the bands with one layer of thin, bonded polyester fleece like Pellon's *Quilter's Fleece*. Apply the bands following the pattern instructions, or bind as shown on page 72. Sew a matching fabric belt. *Optional*: Channel-quilt the band and belt with straight-stitching, every 1/2".

References: *Knit, Serge & Sew* videotape and transcript ©1987 from Nancy's Notions, Ltd.; *Owner's Guide to Sewing Machines, Sergers and Knitting Machines*, by Gale Grigg Hazen, ©1989 Chilton Book Co.; *Proper Proportions, Machine Knit Drafting the Easy Way*, © 1988 by Lannie Rae Aasen, available from Knots & Knits, 1006 N.E. Salsman Rd., Corbett, OR 97019 for $9.95 postpaid; and *Serging Sweaters*, by Naomi Baker, ©1988, *Update Newsletters* (for addresses not listed here, see "References," pages 174-177).

7. Dressed-up Serging

We're continually surprised by the number of avid serger enthusiasts who've never tried dressy fabrics and garments. What a waste. You and your serger can make short work out of seaming and finishing silks, silkies, sheers, and laces. You'll glean new shortcuts, thanks to fast, delicate serging, and be the best-dressed at the next special occasion.

Basic Strategies

Serge Inconspicuous Seams

Lightweight serger, machine embroidery, lingerie, and #80 nylon filament threads are best for fine silks, silkies, sheers, and laces. Always change to a new, fine needle to prevent snagging and needle holes in delicate fabrics.

If the bodice and lining will be seamed together, *serge-finish edges together before straight-stitching*, then press open (see Fig. 7-1). Sheers and

BODICE LINING

SERGE FINISH, STRAIGHT STITCH & PRESS OPEN.

Fig. 7-1

laces can be seamed beautifully with the narrow rolled edge (Fig. 7-2). Test

Fig. 7-2

stitch length and threads on garment scraps to achieve maximum durability without sacrificing softness. *Is puckering a problem?* Shorten the stitch length increments; the needle tension may also need to be loosened slightly.

☞ **Update tip:** Serge and sew all long skirt seams in the same direction (generally waistline to hem) so that the garment will hang smoothly and evenly.

Minimize Bulk

For the smoothest fit, bulk should be minimized. (The flatter the finish, the better.) For lace-trimmed edges, serge-finish the edge first, then apply the lace (Fig. 7-3). The lace trim can be secured

Fig. 7-3

with topstitching, or if using the melt adhesive thread (see page 40) in the upper looper, by simply fusing. (For shaped lace edgings, look for scalloped trim or clip apart a galloon, a lace that's scalloped along each lengthwise edge.)

☞ **Update tip:** Bridal specialist Ann Beyer makes gown bodices facingless by glue-basting the lining and fabric together (Fig. 7-4), serge-finishing, and then lapping and topstitching the edge trim or lace.

GLUE & SERGE FINISH.

THEN, TOPSTITCH TRIM.

Fig. 7-4

Narrow-rolled edges solve the bulk problem beautifully. Use this lightweight hem finish for skirt tiers and ruffled flounces; no other hemming is required. Be careful to lengthen

SERGED RUFFLES:

stitches for more delicate finishing (unless a heavier, decorative finish is desired). If raveling is a problem, widen the stitch bite (see how-to's on pages 136-137).

Custom Finishes

• **Create serged lace.** Fabricate this looped trim on ruffles, hemlines, tucks, and collars. Adjust for the widest width, longest length 3/4-thread (if possible) or 3-thread stitch. Use lightweight serger thread in the loopers and #80 monofilament thread in the needle(s).

1. Serge-finish the edge.

2. Serge one row of stitching to the fabric, *allowing all but the needleline to hang off the edge* (see Fig. 7-5).

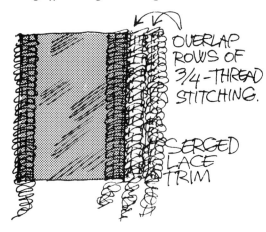

OVERLAP ROWS OF 3/4-THREAD STITCHING.

SERGED LACE TRIM

Fig. 7-5

3. Overlap the next row, positioning the needleline(s) *just inside the loops of the previous row*. Repeat until the desired lace trim width is achieved. *Optional:* To ruffle the serged lace, stretch as shown. See Fig. 7-6.

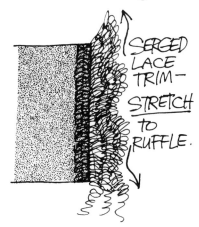

SERGED LACE TRIM— STRETCH to RUFFLE.

Fig. 7-6

• **Embellish with beaded piping,** a lovely accent at neckline, princess, and waistline seams. Create by serging fine pearl, bead, or sequin strands to a folded strip of 1 1/4"-wide organza or *Seams Great®* (Fig. 7-7); refer to "Serging Bead Strands," page 63. For piping application tips, see page 56.

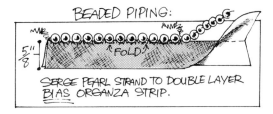

BEADED PIPING:

5/8"

"FOLD"

SERGE PEARL STRAND TO DOUBLE LAYER BIAS ORGANZA STRIP.

Fig. 7-7

• **Trace tulle or illusion** for veils, headpieces, accessories, and accents. (Tracing is simply serge-finishing with a narrow rolled edge stitch.) Experiment with different threads—rayon in the upper looper adds shine, whereas woolly stretch nylon provides denser coverage and a matte finish. Shortening the stitch length will intensify the color contrast of the tracing. Serge over fishing line and stretch the edge to flounce the tracing (see pages 60-62).

TRACED TULLE

Serged Glitz

Lamé is a lightweight fabric woven with metallic filaments in one direction and extra-fine colored threads in the other. Because the metal fiber is very slippery, lamé ravels easily. (Some lamés are fused to a very soft tricot backing to control the raveling problem. These bonded lamés can be routinely serge-seamed.)

ROLLED EDGES

ROLLED EDGE

THAT MIDAS TOUCH IN GOLD LAMÉ

Unbonded lamé, the more readily available type, requires stitch-testing. Set the serged stitch at the maximum width and a rather short stitch length—about 2 mm. Serge sample seams lengthwise, crosswise, and on the bias. Pull against the seams, stressing the stitching, to test for durability and thread slippage; the results will tell you if and when you need to reinforce the needleline of serged seams with a conventional straight-stitch.

A ruffled style is a good candidate for light-catching lamé. *The narrow rolled edge will finish the ruffles beautifully, if you serge in the grain direction across the metal filaments,* parallel to the fine colored threads. If you stitch in the other direction—oops!—the rolled edge will promptly pull away from the fabric. To camouflage stitches, consider using matching, blending metallic-colored or #80 nylon filament thread in the upper looper.

☞ **Update tip:** Combine fine metallic thread with woolly stretch nylon (in the upper looper) for better strength and edge coverage. When using double strands, tension will need to be loosened to facilitate uniform feeding.

Remember: Metallic sewing threads are fragile, so *slow down your serging speed to prevent breakage.* Because they are wiry and resist rolling, the metal fibers of the lamé may poke out between the rolled edge stitches. Increase the cutting bite of your serger slightly beyond the normal setting; instructions are given on pages 136-137. The fabric will roll under farther, and hence, you'll have fewer "pokies." Or align a strip of *Seams Great®* (bias-cut sheer tricot) on the top edge of the fabric. Stitch the rolled edge through both layers. The tricot wraps invisibly around the fabric edge (under the stitches) and smoothly rolls under the metal fibers. Trim away the excess *Seams Great®* right next to the serging.

Glitter-flecked tapestry can make a wonderful jacket to pair with skirts and pants already in your wardrobe. Test-stitch on fabric scraps to determine if serger seaming is appropriate. Would conventional pressed-open seams be less bulky? For decorative edge finishing, thread the upper looper with a metallic yarn like *Candlelight* from YLI. If the jacket is unlined, consider finishing interior seam and facing edges decoratively with a lightweight metallic (as long as it's not too scratchy) or rayon thread.

Sequins demand special handling, but the results are spectacular. Select a style with a minimum number of seams. *Before stitching any seams, remove all sequins from the seam allow-*

ances. Serging over even one pesky disk breaks needles every time. Instead of snipping the joining threads, snip the sequins. Threads remain intact to hold the other sequins securely. Simply cut a pie-wedge from each sequin—from the outer edge to the center hole—and use serger tweezers to slip the sequin out of its holding stitch. See Fig. 7-8.

SNIP SEQUINS AWAY IN SEAM ALLOWANCES WITHOUT CUTTING THREADS.

Fig. 7-8

Instant glitzy accents: With lamé scarves, you can glamorize basics like business suits and knit separates. Use lamés, silks, chiffons, and any other

INSTANT SERGED GLITZ!

METALLIC EDGED:

OBLONG SCARF

LACE HANKIE

METALLIC SERGED BRAID SCROLLWORK

lightweight dressy fabrics. Serge-finish the edges with shiny, metallic thread or invisible nylon and a narrow rolled or balanced stitch. Or, for a shawl, choose a glitter-flecked tapestry, and flatlock-fringe with all-purpose or shiny rayon thread (see page 115 of *Creative Serging Illustrated*). Create couched scrollwork (see page 57) out of serged metallic braid to embellish a wide-waisted belt.

FLAT-LOCKED FRINGED GLITTER TAPESTRY SHAWL

8. Fast-Serged Accessories

It's no secret that accessories can make or break an outfit. But ready-made accessories can break your budget. Serge instead. These super easy-to-make sashes, belts, scarves, and stoles require minimal materials and sewing time.

Twist-to-Fit Sash

This tucked and twisted sash, a copy of a bestselling ready-made, is instantly *Velcro*®-adjustable to comfortably fit any 25-35" waistline. It calls for only fabric scraps and an hour or less of sewing time; straight-stitching attaches the *Velcro*® tape and decorative serging finishes the sash edges. Sew

several for yourself, then start checking off your holiday gift list. For summer accessorizing, use cotton Madras or linen. For fall accents, try a silky foulard print or synthetic suede. In fancy brocade or satin, this versatile belt adds just the right touch of elegance for evening dressing.

Materials Needed

• **Fashion fabric.** One piece 3" wide by 41" long (less than 1/8 yard of 45"-wide fabric). See Fig. 8-1.

• **Lining.** One piece 3" wide by 41" long (if the fashion fabric is light-weight, it can be used for the lining piece). See Fig. 8-1.

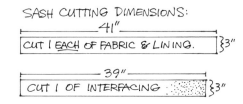

SASH CUTTING DIMENSIONS:
41"
CUT 1 EACH OF FABRIC & LINING. 3"

39"
CUT 1 OF INTERFACING 3"

Fig. 8-1

• **Interfacing.** One piece 3" wide by 39" long. See Fig. 8-3. Use a sew-in, nonwoven interfacing like *Pellon 910 Sew-In for Feather to Midweight Fabrics.*

• *Velcro®* **or other hook and loop fastener tape.** Two pieces: one of the loop tape, 3/4" wide by 20" long, and another of the hook tape, 3/4" wide by 2-1/2".

• **Decorative thread.** One cone or spool of topstitching, woolly stretch nylon, pearl cotton, metallic, or rayon thread (for upper looper). Select two spools or cones of all-purpose or serger thread to blend with the fashion fabric and decorative thread (for the lower looper and needle).

• **Gluestick.** Substitute for pins (only if the fabric doesn't water spot).

How-to's

1. On the right side of the lining, place two 10" lengths of loop tape 4 1/2" in from each end and centered (Fig. 8-2). Baste in place with gluestick. Straight-stitch around the edges of the tape.

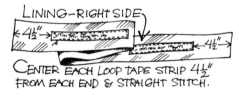

Fig. 8-2

2. On the short ends of the fashion fabric and lining pieces, fold under 1/2" to the wrong side. Gluestick-baste in place.

3. To layer and align the sash pieces, place the lining on a flat surface wrong side up, position the interfacing on the lining, and place the fashion fabric on the interfacing, right side up. Pin or gluestick the long edges together. See Fig. 8-3.

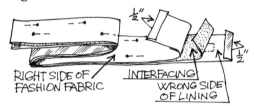

Fig. 8-3

4. Thread your serger. Use decorative thread in the upper looper; use all-purpose or serger thread in the needle and lower looper. Adjust for a 3-thread balanced stitch. (For tips on testing and adjusting for decorative serging, see Chapter 4, pages 40-46.)

5. Serge the long edges of the sash, right side up. Trim off 1/8" as you serge. Leave a 1-1/2" thread chain tail at each end. Tuck the thread chain tails inside the sash end openings. See Fig. 8-4.

TRIM ⅛" DECORATIVE SERGER STITCH.
TUCK THREAD TAILS INSIDE SASH ENDS.

Fig. 8-4

6. Make a tuck at each end of the sash. Fold the fabric as shown in Fig. 8-5. Pin or machine baste. The finished end should measure about 1-1/4".

7. On the outside of the sash, place a 1-1/4" strip of hook tape at each end (on top of the tuck). Straight-stitch around the edges of the tape. See Fig. 8-5. Press the sash.

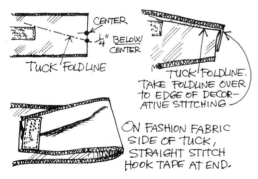

CENTER
¼" BELOW CENTER
TUCK FOLDLINE

TUCK FOLDLINE.
TAKE FOLDLINE OVER TO EDGE OF DECORATIVE STITCHING

ON FASHION FABRIC SIDE OF TUCK, STRAIGHT STITCH HOOK TAPE AT END.

Fig. 8-5

8. Adjust the sash to fit in front by attaching the right hook tape end to the left loop tape strip, and the left hook tape end to the right loop tape strip, as shown on page 83.

Serged Ribbing Rose

Ribbing roses are the latest accessory rage and are a cinch to serge.

1. Cut a 3" by 20" piece of ribbing (the greatest stretch should parallel the longer side). See Fig. 8-6. (Simulate

Fig. 8-6

the rose shape with finger-gathering before proceeding to the next step; narrow and/or shorten the ribbing to achieve the rose size desired. *Generally, it's best to start with a smaller piece if using heavier-weight ribbing.)*

2. To make a lettuce-leaf finish along one long edge of the ribbing, satin serge-finish with a rolled hem, stretching the edge as you serge. (Experiment on scraps first, so you can refine the stitch width and length. Also, for neater finishing, the bite may require widening (see pages 136-137.) Taper the end (Fig. 8-7).

Fig. 8-7

3. Along the other long edge, serge over heavy thread; pull the heavy thread to gather into a rose shape. See Fig. 8-8. Use the heavy thread tail to hand sew the back of the rose together and secure a jewelry or safety pin.

Fig. 8-8

Variations: For a heftier rose, cut, serge-finish, and *gather two layers of ribbing* (wrong sides together). Also, Gail prefers serge-finishing the straight side of the ribbing and serge-gathering the tapered side, which results in a flatter, more flared rose.

Pocket Squares

Four-in-One

Packing and keeping track of small accessories can be a pain. Simplify by replacing four pocket squares with one that's multicolored. Serge together 6" squares of silk or silk-like fabric into a 12" pocket handkerchief. See Fig. 8-9. (It's likely your stash inventory includes some lovely hanky-makings.)

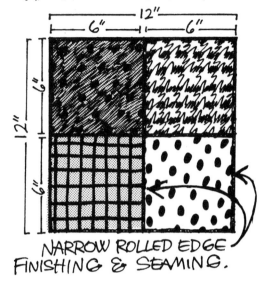

Fig. 8-9

Seam and finish the edges with 3-thread rolled-edge hemming; try using woolly stretch nylon in the upper looper and the finest (#80) monofilament in the needle and lower looper. Keep the stitch length long enough for a delicate finish and lightweight seams. Seam two sets of two each, then seam the two halves together.

☞ **Update tip:** Rounding the corners slightly will prevent the corners from becoming too pointed (see page 114, Fig. 11-2).

Place the hanky in a jacket pocket, exposing whichever corner catches your fancy that day. In better men's departments, similar "wardrobe-in-one" silk squares can cost as much as $30.00. Serge several—for you and for those fortunate enough to be on your gift list.

Solid-Color Hankies

Soften menswear-styled or dress-for-success suit jackets by placing a feminine hanky in the chest pocket. Cut 10" or 12" squares of silk, silk-like, or lace fabric. Finish the edges with a matching or contrasting color using a narrow rolled hemming.

Quick Knit Accessories

Knit accessories willingly contour and drape, updating any wardrobe with shapely accents. These soft scarves, belts, and wraps make sewing sense, too. They can be serged and straight-stitched in minutes using scraps or remnants, and they cost much less than their trendy ready-made cousins. All you do is cut out and edge-finish basic shapes; when worn, the shapes drape, fold, wrap, and tie to fit and flatter.

The technique for edge-finishing is simple, but it looks very professional. First, serge-finish the raw edges with medium-length, medium-to-wide width balanced serging (either 2- or 3-thread). Turn raw edges 5/8" to the wrong side and twin-needle topstitch 3/8" from the fold (Fig. 8-10).

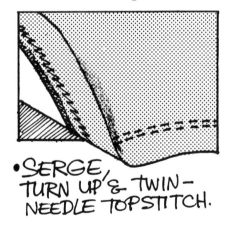

• SERGE, TURN UP & TWIN-NEEDLE TOPSTITCH.

Fig. 8-10

36" SCARF AS A HEAD WRAP

36" SCARF AS NECKLINE ACCENT.

72" SIZE AS SHAWL

Triangles

Rather than the usual square folded in half, knit triangles make less cumbersome scarve when sewn single-layer. Two 36" triangles, sized for **head wraps and neckline accents,** can be cut from a mere yard of wide-width knit. Or, serge-seam the triangles together (Fig. 8-11) to make an oversized 72" shawl triangle, ample enough for lavish draping over a dress, suit, or coat.

When the 72" triangle is wrapped and tied around the waist, it becomes skirtlike, creating a slimmer silhouette and a "new" outfit. For the smaller scarves, fabric favorites include interlocks and jerseys; for the larger seamed shawls, choose doubleknits and interlocks without discernible right and wrong sides.

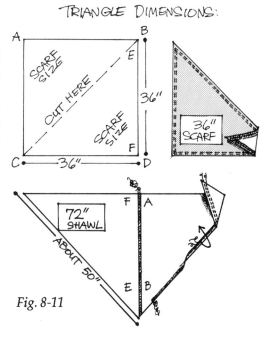

TRIANGLE DIMENSIONS:

SCARF SIZE

CUT HERE

SCARF SIZE

36"

36"

36" SCARF

72" SHAWL

ABOUT 50"

Fig. 8-11

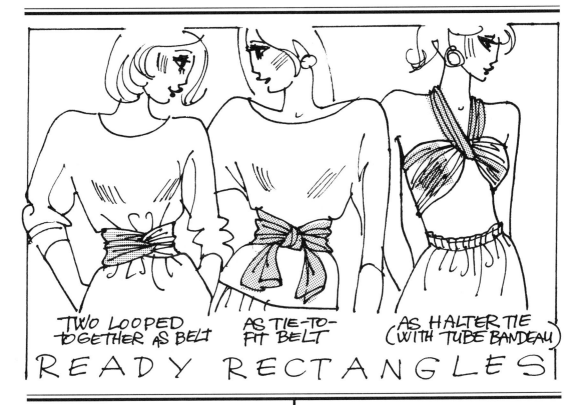

TWO LOOPED TOGETHER AS BELT

AS TIE-TO-FIT BELT

AS HALTER TIE (WITH TUBE BANDEAU)

READY RECTANGLES

Rectangles

Touted as **head wraps, sashes, and ties,** knit rectangles (typically called sashes) retail for $10 and are sewn precisely as described here.

Simply cut out a rectangle and edge-finish it (Fig. 8-12). Longer rectangles are required for braiding, so either

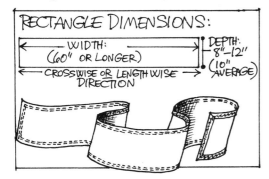

RECTANGLE DIMENSIONS:

WIDTH: (60" OR LONGER)

DEPTH: 8"–12" (10" AVERAGE)

CROSSWISE OR LENGTHWISE DIRECTION

Fig. 8-12

make seams to piece or cut the width in the lengthwise direction. For rectangular tubes that can also be worn as **leggings,** double the depth; fit; seam in a circle; and edge-finish the short ends. Thinner knits for sashes—singleknits, jerseys, interlocks— can be braided, twisted, and knotted without adding bulk.

☞ **Update tip:** For smooth fastening, try threading rectangle and triangle ends through belt buckles, instead of tying or knotting.

Sources: If you are unable to find twin needles locally, contact these mail-order firms: Aardvark Adventures, Clotilde, Nancy's Notions, Serge and Sew Notions, or the Sewing Emporium (for addresses, see "Serge-by-Mail Directory," pages 163-173).

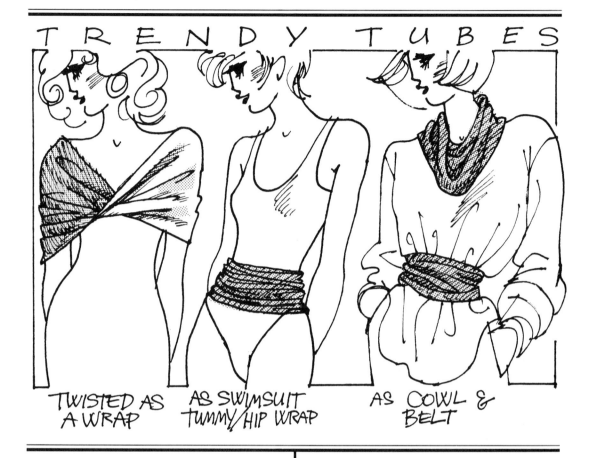

TRENDY TUBES

TWISTED AS A WRAP

AS SWIMSUIT TUMMY/HIP WRAP

AS COWL & BELT

Tubes

Popularized by the Units System's modulars craze, this accessory shape is incredibly versatile as a **belt, hip wrap, cowl, hood, headband, and bandeau.** The knit tube's biggest selling point remains its ability to hold shape and position, comfortably, without belt loops or constant adjusting. Clever designers and coordinators are now developing new fashion applications for this practical accessory. Why not add color accent and tummy-trimming camouflage to your basic tanksuit or leotard with a Lycra®-blend tube? Or wear a large, long, twisted tube as an evening wrap? How about transforming a tunic into a shorter blouson with a tube hip wrap?

Cut out following the guidelines given in Fig. 8-13. *Allow at least 4" more*

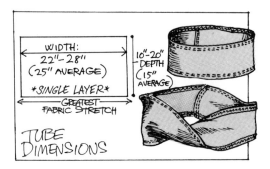

Fig. 8-13

in width to compensate for twisted styles. Remember that tube-sewing is not an exact science; dimensions vary with fit preferences and the stretchability of the fabric type used. After cutting out, fit (adjusting the width and depth), seam, and edge-finish. Twisted styles must be twisted before seaming. The wrong side will be exposed on portions of twisted styles, but the drape of the tube will handily conceal the edge finishing.

☞ **Update tip:** For an instantly reversible, twisted tube, *simply place one tube inside another the same size, wrong sides together.* Twist to reveal the other color. (There will be two twists in the tube rather than just the one which occurs when the tube is twisted before it's seamed.)

Stretchy cotton or cotton-blend interlocks are the most prevalent choices for tubes, but sweaterknits, jerseys, and Lycra® blends shouldn't be ruled out. Dig through your stash and you'll discover intriguing materials for tube-making.

Quick Serged Cover-up

We worked with expert serger seamstress Naomi Baker to come up with this wrap-to-fit cover-up (see page 93), which can be worn as a skirt or a strapless dress. The finishing, easing, and seaming are all serged for convenient, efficient, one-machine sewing.

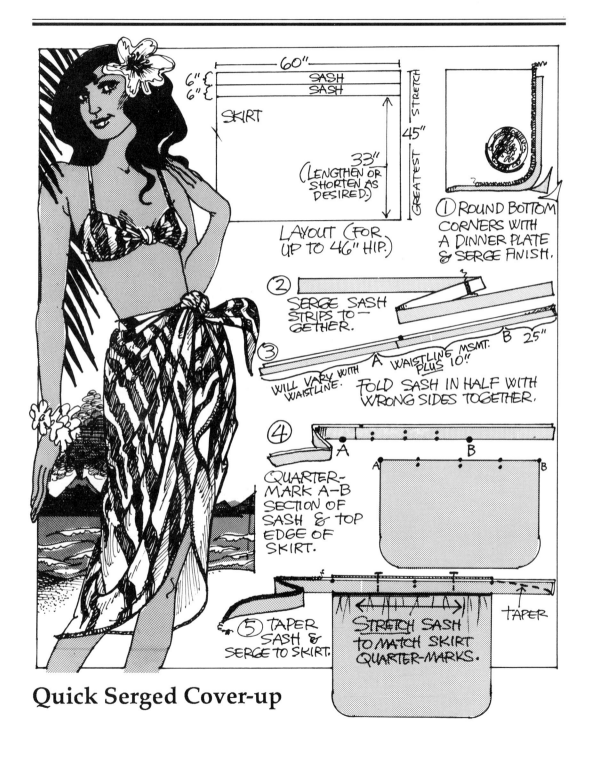

60"

6" ∫ SASH
6" ∫ SASH

SKIRT

45" GREATEST STRETCH

33"
(LENGTHEN OR SHORTEN AS DESIRED.)

LAYOUT (FOR UP TO 46" HIP.)

① ROUND BOTTOM CORNERS WITH A DINNER PLATE & SERGE FINISH.

② SERGE SASH STRIPS TO- GETHER.

③ A WAISTLINE MSMT. PLUS 10" B 25"
WILL VARY WITH WAISTLINE.
FOLD SASH IN HALF WITH WRONG SIDES TOGETHER.

④ QUARTER- MARK A-B SECTION OF SASH & TOP EDGE OF SKIRT.

A B

A B

TAPER

⑤ TAPER SASH & SERGE TO SKIRT.

STRETCH SASH TO MATCH SKIRT QUARTER-MARKS.

Quick Serged Cover-up

9. Maximum Efficiency, Minimal Time: Production-Order Serging

The few minutes you spend mulling over construction order can save hours of sewing time. Plus, you'll produce a more professional garment. During this strategy stage, you can streamline the process, consolidating tasks that require the same serging stitch and thereby minimize machine adjustments and rethreading. It also helps to determine which machine—your serger or your conventional machine—is the best tool for each step. Nearly every garment calls for integration of the two technologies (called "tandem sewing"or "dual construction"), but *limiting movements back and forth between the two machines maximizes efficiency, speed, and sewing satisfaction.*

Planning Considerations and Questions:

• **Serge continuously.** Serge-finish and serge-seam at one sitting. Because the presser foot doesn't need to be raised, several edges can be serged without cutting threads between.

• **Serge and sew "in the flat."** For easiest handling, sewing, and pressing, complete as many steps on a flat unit as possible before it is seamed in or to a circle.

• **Group similar steps and stitches.** Do as much of each task— serge-seaming, serge-finishing (like narrow hemming), straight-stitching or pressing— as possible before proceeding to the next task.

• **Which type of seaming methods are best? Where?** If the seam will be pressed open, the serge-finishing is completed before any of the seams are straight-stitched. (Zippers in garments generally call for pressed-open seams.)

• **How will the sleeves be sewn in—flat or in a circle?** Check the sleeve pattern piece. A flatter sleeve cap is easier to serge in, but with a little more pinning and at a slower pace, even curved caps are possible. If you do serge-seam the sleeve in a circle, simply overlap the beginning and ending stitches (Fig. 9-1).

Fig. 9-1

• **How will the neckline be finished?** As in most factory-made blouses and shirts, the back facing can usually be replaced with a serged seam. See Fig. 9-5 on page 96.

Implementing Basic Plans

The following plans for a basic one-piece dress, tie blouse, and four-panel skirt can be easily modified to work for your style and fabric.

Basic One-Piece Dress
1. **Serge-finish** the center back seam edges.

2. **Straight-stitch** the center front and back seams. **Press** the center back seam open. **Straight-stitch** the center back zipper application. See Fig. 9-2.

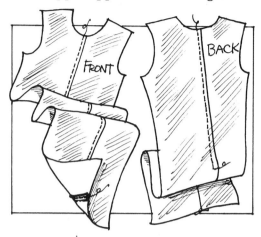

Fig. 9-2

3. **Serge-finish** the center front seam edges together. **Press** to one side and **topstitch.** See Fig. 9-2.

4. **Straight-stitch** the shoulder seams of the dress and facings. **Press** the facing seams open.

5. **Serge-finish** the shoulder seams and facing edge, continuously, as shown (Fig. 9-3). Also, **straight-stitch** the side seams. **Serge-finish** the edges together.

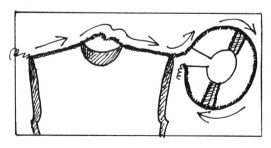

Fig. 9-3

6. **Serge-seam** the sleeves.

7. **Straight-stitch** the sleeves into the dress. Serge-finish the seam edges together.

8. **Serge-finish** the hem edge. Turn up and topstitch.

Basic Tie Blouse
(illustration, page 97)

1. **Serge-seam and serge-finish** the tie with a narrow rolled edge (Fig. 9-4).

Fig. 9-4

2. **Serge-finish** the sleeve placket openings. (A placket will not be sewn to the opening.) (See Fig. 9-8.)

3. **Adjust** for a medium-width and medium-length balanced serger stitch.

4. **Serge** the shoulder seams.

5. **Serge-finish** the facing edges.

6. **Serge-seam** the neckline (Fig. 9-5).

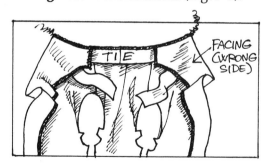

Fig. 9-5

7. **Serge-seam** the sleeves to the bodice armholes (Fig. 9-6).

8. **Serge** the sleeve and side seams (Fig. 9-6).

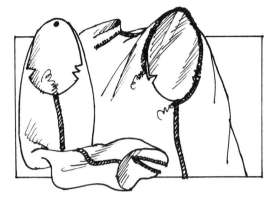

Fig. 9-6

9. **Serge** the cuff seams (Fig. 9-7); serge

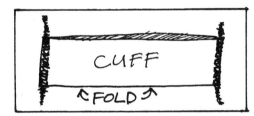

Fig. 9-7

the cuffs to the sleeves (Fig. 9-8).

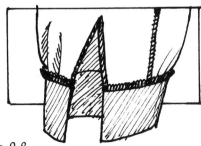

Fig. 9-8

10. With a conventional sewing machine, **topstitch,** then **sew** buttonholes and buttons.

Basic Four-Panel Skirt

1. **Serge-finish** the seam edges continuously and the unnotched edge of the waistband (Fig. 9-9).

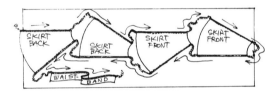

Fig. 9-9

2. With a conventional sewing machine, **straight-stitch** the center front

and back seams. **Press** the seams open. **Straight-stitch** the zipper application. See Fig. 9-10.

Fig. 9-10

3. **Straight-stitch** the side seams.

4. **Serge-finish** the hem edge (Fig. 9-11).

Fig. 9-11

5. **Straight-stitch** the unfinished edge of the waistband to the skirt. **Straight-stitch** the waistband ends, fold over, and stitch-in-the-ditch to secure.

6. **Turn up and topstitch** the hem.

Basic 30-Minute Slacks

With our speedy serging strategies, you can sew slacks in less time than it would take to wash and press a pair.

Suitable Patterns

Every pattern company offers styles well-suited for fast serging knits and/or wovens. Look for a pocketless pant with a pull-on elastic waistline.

The Best Fabrics

Choose a mid-weight knit or woven fabric, like wool jersey, cotton interlock, double knit, rayon challis, or lightweight linen and wool. For a more casual pant, mid-weight denim or chambray would also be advisable.

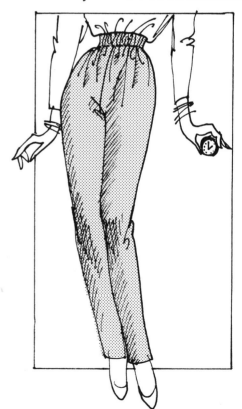

Fast Fitting

Alter before cutting out. Generally, alterations are minimal because pull-on pants are cut fuller through the hips. If using a woven, the hipline finished measurement should be at least 4" larger than your hips. For interlock knits, hipline ease isn't required; for more stable double knits, allow at least 1". To allow you to pull the pants on and off with ease, *the waistline should be at least as big as your hip measurement.*

Groundwork

• Set up your ironing board close to your serger and sewing machine.

• Change to a twin needle in your sewing machine and use thread that matches the slacks.

• If you're confident about the fit, consider serging several pair at one sitting. Follow the sewing order in sequence for each pair; for instance, serge all the outseams, then serge-finish all the waistline and hem edges (Steps 2 and 3, below). (Following this factory-production method, it's likely that your sewing time per pant will be less than 30 minutes.)

• *Fold the fabric right sides together* for the pattern layout. Use weights to secure the pattern and a rotary cutter to cut out. You'll be ready to serge and press after cutting out.

• To save time, learn to finger-pin to match seamlines for accurate seaming. Use the presser foot to secure the outseam layers at the waistline (Fig. 9-12). Then, grasp the outseam at the midpoint and hem. Serge, releasing at the finger-pin positions.

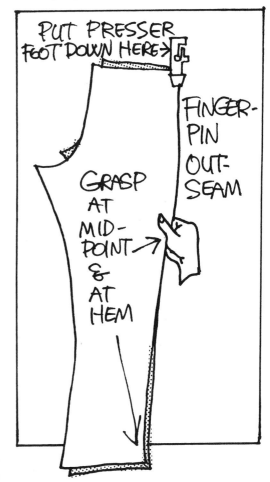

Fig. 9-12

Speediest Ten-Step Sewing and Serging Order

✎ **Note:** When directions are given for one pant piece, side, or leg, repeat the same procedure for the other corresponding piece.

1. **Fold** each pant piece wrong sides together and **press to crease** from the hem to the crotchline.

2. **Finger-pin** the outseam of a front piece to a back piece. Serge directionally, from the waistline to the hem edge. See Fig. 9-12.

3. **Serge-finish** the waistline and hemline edges, securing the outseam toward the back pant piece. **Press** the seam. See Fig. 9-13.

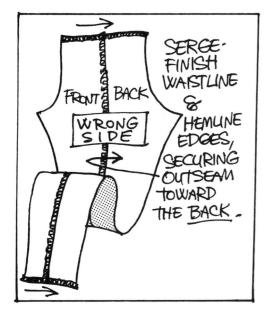

Fig. 9-13

4. **Press** the hem and casing allowances to the wrong side.

5. **Finger-pin** the inseam. **Serge** directionally, from the crotch to the hem edge.

6. **Serge** the crotch seam. Alternate inseam direction to decrease bulk. See Fig. 9-14.

Fig. 9-14

7. **Press** the inseams.

8. **Apply** the elastic. Fit the elastic to your waist. Choose from either of these popular casing methods:

• **Sew the elastic in a circle,** by overlapping 1/2" and topstitching. Fold the casing over the elastic circle and edge-stitch next to the serged finishing to create the casing. See Fig. 9-15.

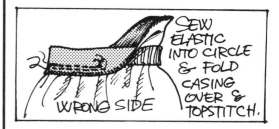

Fig. 9-15

• **Or, sew the elastic into a circle after inserting it in the casing.** Leave an opening for the elastic adjustment and sewing. Pull the ends through the opening. Fit, overlap, topstitch, and sew the opening closed. (If your weight tends to fluctuate, leave the opening and simply safety pin the elastic into a circle.) See Fig. 9-16.

Fig. 9-16

👉 **Update tip:** Stretch & Sew founder, Ann Person, teaches a variation of the second method. *She doesn't cut the elastic, but marks the waistline measurement and leaves it on the roll* so that the casing doesn't have to be gathered as you stitch. After inserting, the elastic is pulled up, cut, overlapped, and topstitched.

9. **Topstitch** the hems.

10. **Change** from the twin needle to a single sewing machine needle. **Try on** the slacks, distributing the waistline ease for the most comfortable and flattering fit. **Stitch-in-the-ditch** of the side seamlines to retain the ease distribution and prevent the elastic from twisting in the casing (Fig. 9-17). Finally, **straight-stitch** to reinforce the crotch seam along the needleline.

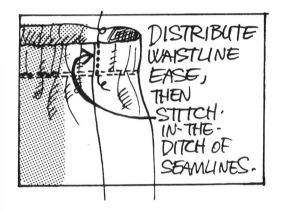

Fig. 9-17

Variations: Copy the latest ready-to-wear waistband look with wide decorative elastic (Fig. 9-18). See page 27. Or, create the trendy paper-bag pull-on waistband. See pages 24-25.

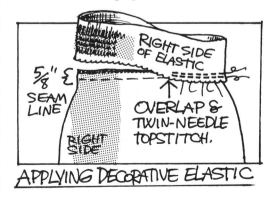

Fig. 9-18

10. Alter, Fit, and Restyle

Got a growing pile of clothes that need to be altered? Join the club. Alter the fast, professional way—with serging. Without spending money on any materials but thread, you'll quickly transform that pile into better fitting, updated wearables.

Rapid Unraveling of Serged Stitches

When it's alteration time, even staunch serger loyalists have been known to curse their beloved machine. Unraveling serged stitches can be frustrating, particularly when you pull the wrong thread and end up with a puckered, tangled mess. The following are three foolproof methods for ridding an edge or seam of serging while keeping your nerves intact.

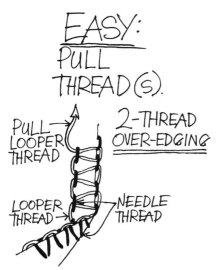

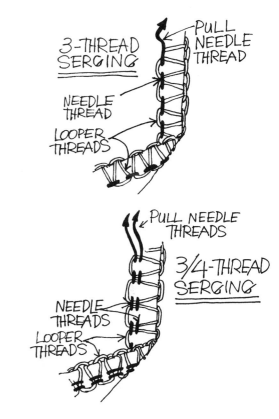

Fig. 10-1

• **Easy:** Pull a thread or threads. On 2-thread overedging, pull the looper thread. On 3- and 3/4-thread overlocking, pull the needle thread(s). On double chainstitching, pull the looper thread (Fig. 10-1).

☞ **Update tip:** Pulling 3-thread or 3/4-thread needle thread(s) also can ease or gather a serged edge. Although there are more effective methods for gathering large areas (see pages 11-13), pulling thread(s) is convenient and quick for easing flared hems on skirts and tablecloths.

• **Easier:** On 2-, 3- and 3/4-thread stitches, simply rip through the looper thread. This technique will also require picking out the clipped threads, but with the exception of very close serging, this shouldn't be too time-consuming (Fig. 10-2).

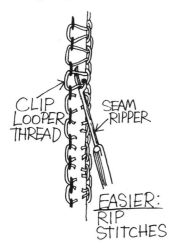

Fig. 10-2

• **Easiest:** Serge or trim off the first row of stitching. For stitchless serge-trimming, pull the thread out of the serger needle(s) (Fig. 10-3).

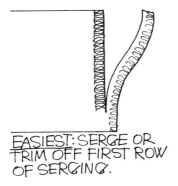

Fig. 10-3

Fine-Tuning Fit

The saying is, *"You can't serge and custom-fit."* To the contrary, serging can streamline fitting. Agreed, you can't let out a standard width 3-thread serged seam (at least not appreciably and maintain durability). However, serging offers unique fitting opportunities not possible with conventional stitching.

• **Practice preventive fitting.** With the fashion pendulum swinging toward more fitted fashions, it's imperative that you ensure an accurate fit before serging, if at all possible. Compare your measurements to the pattern's, then alter accordingly. Allow for comfort and design ease; most comprehensive sewing books include ease charts that will serve as guidelines (or refer to page 151 of *Creative Serging Illustrated*).

During the recent fashion seasons we've grown accustomed to loose, oversized fit. You may have compensated by buying a smaller pattern or by buying your regular size, even though you've gained weight or inches. (Patterns described as "very loose fitting" can have as much as 15" of design ease built in.) *Beware:* Close-fitting styles are infiltrating the fashion scene, and it's crucial that you reevaluate your pattern size (and those of the people you sew for).

Allow 1" seam allowances if you're at all uncertain about the pattern fit, even after measuring. This fitting insurance compensates for any inaccurate measuring or unforeseen weight gains between cutting out and sewing the garment. After pin- or baste-fitting, seams can be serged.

- **Baste the super-fast serged way.** All you do is loosen the needle tension. With a gentle tug on the needle thread tail, it should effortlessly slip out of the stitch formation, simultaneously releasing the looper threads (Fig. 10-4). Put serge-basting to work and you'll spend

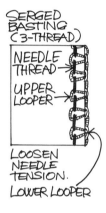

Fig. 10-4

less time alternating between your serger and conventional machine.

Caution: Skim straying threads only, not the seam width (you may need room if the garment is closely fitted). After checking the fit and pulling out the basting, tighten the needle tension and serge the seam. Or, if the garment must be taken in, don't even bother pulling out the serged basting. Just serge off the seam.

- **Take in serged seams by serging a new, deeper seam** (see Fig. 10-3 on page 103). How did we ever survive without this timesaving tapering technique? It's indispensable for knit slacks (convert pull-ons into tighter-fitting leggings), men's shirts (taper from the underarm down, serging off the flatfelled seam, if there is one), and sweaters (a more slenderizing silhouette can be created by serge-tapering the sleeves and bulk at the underarm (see "Better Sweaters for Less," pages 107). To blend the start and finish of the new seam, taper out and into the original seam, aligning the needlelines for maximum smoothness.

- **Serge-finish conventional seam allowance edges to prevent raveling and to facilitate letting out** (Fig. 10-5).

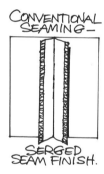

Fig. 10-5

Many serger owners limit their technique repertoire to serge-seaming and forget the pleasures (and alterability) of pressed-open seams. Controversy continues about when seams should be serge-finished. Some argue that allowances must be serged after seaming for accurate gauging of the allowance width, even though maneuvering the seamed fabric can be tricky. Most dressmakers serge all the longer, exposed seam edges (side, center front and back, shoulder seams) right after removing the pattern tissue; these pros opt for the cleaner, ravel-free edges that better withstand the rigors of fitting sessions.

• **Flatlock to let out seams in ravel-free fabrics.** Because seam edges are butted, you gain twice the seam width allowance for extra ease (Fig. 10-6).

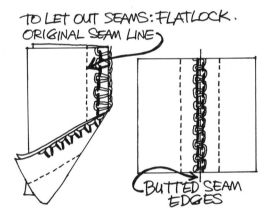

Fig. 10-6

For example, flatlocking a 5/8" seam should yield 3/4"-1" extra ease along each seamline, depending on the overlock stitch width. Stable knits are well-suited for flatlocking: let out a jersey pull-on skirt or a sweatshirt that should be roomier.

☞ **Update tip:** Flatlocking is not recommended for seams that will be subjected to stress or for ravel-prone fabrics. Due to the nature of the flat-lock stitch—no tight needleline or seam allowances—it is inherently weaker than a standard overlocked seam. For added durability, fuse a 1/2" to 1" strip of fusible tricot like Easy-Knit; center it along the wrong side of the flatlocked seam.

• **Let down hems the full depth and serge-finish.** Salvage or recycle any too-short garment. It's the best option when lengthening pleated or flared skirts to the max. (Wide hem facing tape adds too much bulk and takes twice the time.) Usually a narrow rolled edge set at a long stitch length keeps the hem lightweight and subtle.

☞ **Update tip:** Often the original hemline crease is permanently faded or worn, a noticeable problem on kids' clothes that have been washed repeatedly. With the same thread used for the bottom edge rolled hemming, flatlock to hide the old hemline.

Instant Alterations

Pants pulled taut across the thighs. Tops strained at the hip and tummy. Dreaded extra pounds are sabotaging the fit of your wardrobe favorites. Sure, you'll eventually pare down. But how do you look and feel your best until then? And how can you possibly alter serged seams? Dig into this bag of alteration tricks. Once you skinny down (let's be positive), it's equally as easy and quick to return the altered garments to their original size.

Let Out Inseams

Most ready-made jeans and slacks are serged continuously through both inseams with a 4/2-thread overlock stitch. Simply pull out the 2-thread chainstitch; once you get it going, the thread will pull out without breaking or ripping. *(The secret is to pull from the fatter end of the stitch toward the narrower end.)* Once the chainstitch is removed, you'll add at least another 3/4" ease to each pant leg, plus lower the crotch the same amount.

Now try on the pants; you may want to let out the inseam only through the trouble areas, not from the knee to the hem. After fitting, straight-stitch along the inside of the 2-thread overedge stitch (Fig. 10-7). Straight-

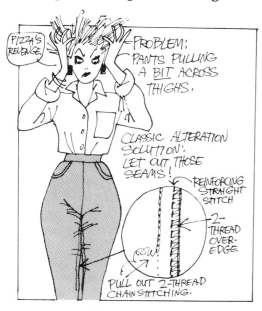

Fig. 10-7

stitching is an important step, because the overedge isn't a seam, but rather a narrow 1/4" finish that will pull open if strained.

Pant-fitting purists may take issue because this alteration throws off the center front crease slightly. However, you will hardly notice the difference; what you will notice is the newfound comfort and flattery of altered pants that skim, not hug, the thighs. When your thighs are thinner, restitch the original chainstitched inseam.

Add Slits

For wearing, sitting, or walking room, add slits. *As much as 4" of extra ease is instantly yours.* Consider slitting blouse and top side seams, straight skirt center back seams, or even the outseams of tapered pants. Open the serging carefully (see pages 102-103), without clipping or damaging the seamline. Try on the garment, marking the slit length desired. Reinforce the seamline end at the top of the slit with straight-stitching. If necessary, take out the hem 2" to 3" on either side of the seamline.

Press the open seam allowances flat to the wrong side; these will be quite narrow if the original seam was serged. To encourage narrow allowances to lie flat, fuse 1"-wide strips of *Easy-Knit* to both wrong sides of the slit, thus securing the edges and adding body. Then, from the right side, secure the allowances with topstitching. Rehem, if necessary. See Fig. 10-8.

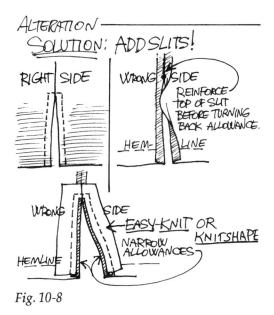

Fig. 10-8

Better Sweaters for Less: Serged Fitting & Restyling

Sweater fit is becoming more body-conscious, moving away from the over-sized shapes of seasons past. This trend is great news for the serger enthusiast, whether a professional dressmaker or home sewer; there's not a garment easier or faster to transform. Altering is budget-wise, too—revamping a sweater you already own is a welcome alternative to paying $80 (and up) for off-the-rack versions.

For prime new project material, shop sales in menswear departments. You'll be amazed by the bargain prices on gorgeous wool, mohair, imported cotton, and even cashmere pullovers and cardigans. (Many colors or styles go on sale in a store because the store's male clientele regards them as too feminine or trendy—perfect for you.) Use the tips and guidelines that follow to alter a new sale "find" or an old favorite.

• **Try the sweater on inside-out.** Use large safety pins to adjust fit. (Straight pins get lost in the thick sweatering or fall out of loosely knit textures.) *Key alterations:* Shorten the bodice and/or take in the side seams and sleeve underarms. See Fig. 10-9.

Fig. 10-9

☞ **Update tip:** Shoulder pads instantly update any sweater. Fit and mark alterations with the pads in place. If you don't have pads for the sweater, make an interchangeable pair. (Machine- or hand-stitch the hook side of *Velcro®* tape to the top side of the pad; the hooks will adhere to any sweater-knit texture.)

• **Adjust your serger to prevent wavy, stretched-out seams and edges.** Lengthen the stitch (4 mm to 5 mm for heavier sweaterings) and widen the stitch to the widest setting. A variety of serger stitches work well, from the most stable 4/2- or 5-thread, to 3/4- or 3-thread overlock. To minimize stretching, use a 2.0 differential feed setting. Or "ease-plus" by force-feeding

the fabric into the foot while holding the fabric layers behind the presser foot. If you ease-plus the seams, straight-stitching first is an unnecessary step (although a reliable one if wavy seams persist).

• **Avoid time-consuming seam-ripping.** Because close fit isn't crucial, just serge another seam, trimming off the original stitching with the serger knives. See Fig. 10-3 on page 103.

• **Limit pressing and overhandling.** When pressing is essential, use only steam, flattening the layers with your hand; cool before moving.

• **Shorten a pull-over sweater** by cutting off the knit-in ribbing, allowing a 1" seam. Cut the sweater to the desired length, allowing a 1" seam on the bodice (Fig. 10-10). Match the mid-

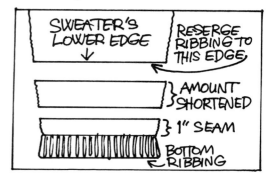

Fig. 10-10

points and side seams of the ribbing and the bodice. With the ribbing on top, re-serge to the bodice, stitching next to (but not through) the ribbing. *Sewn-on ribbing should not be stretched out. Keep it in the relaxed position, and the bodice will automatically ease to fit the ribbing* (see Fig. 6-7 on page 72).

☞ **Update tip:** When shortening moves the bottom edge ribbing closer to the waistline, the ribbing may need to be taken in. Take deeper seam(s) in the ribbing before reapplying to the sweater bodice.

• **Shorten a cardigan with pockets** by cutting the sweater above the pockets. You or your customer will revel in the more slenderizing, pocketless silhouette. *Optional:* Add one or two buttonholes uniformly spaced above the others. Matching buttons can be recycled from the cut-off section.

• **Create the new cropped length** by cutting off the sweater to the desired length plus a 1 1/2" hem. Serge-finish the hem edge. Turn up the finished edge and topstitch 1" from the hemline. Or, after cutting off ribbing, turn up hem, flatlock in place, and pull flat.

☞ **Update tip:** Sweater dresses are typically a one-season look, and they can be unflattering. Extend the dress's fashion life and appeal by hemming to cropped-top length. The leftover sweaterknit can be recycled into accessories (see "Serged Ribbing Rose," page 85).

• **Convert a ribbed turtleneck to a crew.** Simply fold the turtleneck down to the desired width, as shown, and pin. See Fig. 10-11. If necessary, trim off some of the turtleneck width so that the new, narrower crew width will lie flat. From the right side of the gar-

Fig. 10-11

ment, stitch-in-the-ditch of the original seamline to secure the crew. Then, from the wrong side, trim and serge-finish the raw edge of the ribbing.

• **Revitalize stretched-out ribbing** by cutting it off, taking a deeper ribbing side seam, and reapplying to the edge. Or, the stretched-out ribbing can be replaced with ribbing that is more resilient. Because color matching is nearly impossible, strive for an attractive contrast.

• **Add *Ultrasuede®* elbow patches** to cover the worn areas or to emulate country chic. Cut 6" by 8" patches from *Ultrasuede®*. Round the edges into an oval shape. Serge-finish the outer edge with a medium-length and medium-width 3-thread stitch. After marking the elbow placement on the sleeve, edge-stitch the patch to the sleeve.

• **Copy a favorite sweater's design line-for-line** if its too-worn condition doesn't warrant restyling. Complete instructions are outlined in *Serging Sweaters*, a booklet written by serger and knit authority Naomi Baker. (See "References," page 175).

Serge Menswear into Women's Wear

Often men's sweaters, slacks, and shirts are more sturdily made and subtly shaded, of better fabrics, and accented with tailoring rarely seen in women's wear. Sizing appears to be the only obstacle.

WOMEN'S WEAR FROM MENSWEAR!

Now, with the help of your serger, you can buy and resize menswear to fit. Just pretend to be shopping for the man (men?) in your life (although this scheme is a bit thinly disguised when you ask to use the dressing room).

• **Sweaters:** Sizing down oversized sweaters is one of the easiest restyling tasks. See "Better Sweaters for Less," pages 107-110.

• **Tops and shirts:** Avoid cuffed-style sleeves that are too long—restyling with this detailing is too time-consuming. Also, changing neckline sizes can be difficult.

Other alterations are a snap. Simply taper side and sleeve seams. Use a standard 3-thread seam, even if the original was flat-felled. No one will ever notice. See Fig. 10-12.

TOPS & SHIRTS:

SIMPLY TAPER SIDE SEAMS & SLEEVES.

Fig. 10-12

Update tip: Try on the shirt before tapering. You may be surprised how little tapering is required, particularly if the fabric is soft and drapeable. Men's silky pajama tops are perfect for loungewear.

• **Sweats:** Taper and shorten sweatshirt tops as you do sweaters. Mark and taper pant inseams as necessary (most sweatpants do not have outseams). See Fig. 10-13. Then, trim off and reapply ribbing as necessary to shorten (Fig. 10-14). Or, trim off ribbing and hem, if you prefer.

REAPPLY RIBBING IF TOO LONG.

Fig. 10-14

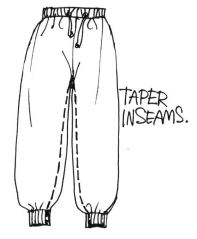

TAPER & SHORTEN TOPS SAME AS FOR SWEATERS.

TAPER INSEAMS.

Fig. 10-13

11. Fabric Decorating— in a Flash

The few hours you invest in decorating with fabric yield uplifting transformations that satisfy season after season. Plus, you bask in the appreciation and admiration of friends and family. Serging has made do-it-yourself decoration easier, faster, and more professional than ever. For this chapter, we've updated our serger methods and compiled our favorites of the newest fabric decorating projects.

Napkin Know-How, Updated

With the rolled hem feature found on most sergers, it's easy to make napkins that rival the best ready-mades, at a fraction of the cost. Quick-change your own table settings or make a gift for a friend. And don't forget to show off your rolled-hem expertise with fancy napkin folds.

Almost any size square works. The most popular napkin sizes are: cocktail (8"-11"), lunch (13"-17"), and dinner (18"-24"). Keep in mind that more elaborate folding schemes require larger napkins.

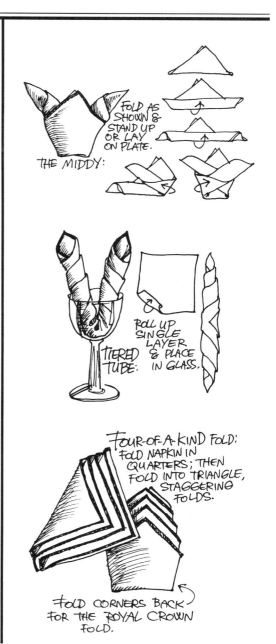

THE MIDDY: FOLD AS SHOWN & STAND UP OR LAY ON PLATE.

TIERED TUBE: ROLL UP SINGLE LAYER & PLACE IN GLASS.

FOUR-OF-A-KIND FOLD: FOLD NAPKIN IN QUARTERS; THEN FOLD INTO TRIANGLE, STAGGERING FOLDS.

FOLD CORNERS BACK FOR THE ROYAL CROWN FOLD.

Materials Needed

- **Napkin fabric.** 1-1/4 yards of 45" width fabric yields sixteen 10" by 10", nine 14" by 14", or four 20" by 20" napkins. For the best rolled hems, use a light- to medium-weight, woven cotton blend. Do not use loosely woven, firm, stiff, or heavy fabrics; the edges won't roll easily. *Optional:* Line napkins with a coordinating fabric and serge -finish as one layer.

- **Thread.** Three cones of nylon filament, size #80 (for the needle and both loopers). Or, two cones of the nylon monofilament (for the needle and lower looper) and one cone of woolly stretch nylon (for the upper looper).

Cutting

Cut the napkins 1" larger than the desired finished size. Hems roll best when the fabric is cut on the grain; however, *when using a print, follow the design line, even if it is slightly off-grain.*

☞ **Update tips:** To mark cutting lines, quickly fold-mark the fabric: trim away selvages, then fold the piece lengthwise into even halves, thirds, or fourths, lengthwise and press. Repeat in the crosswise direction, folding and pressing. Unfolded, the squares will be marked for cutting out. Fig. 11-1.

Fig. 11-1

Or, alternately, cut out and serge-finish simultaneously, instead of cutting out individual squares. For more durable corners, finish all lengthwise grain directions first, then finish the crosswise edges.

Serged Rolled-Hem Checklist

1. Adjust for 3-thread narrow rolled hemming. Follow your serger owner's manual.

2. Adjust for a short stitch length: 1-1.5 mm.

3. Adjust for a narrow stitch width - about 2-2.5 mm. (On some sergers, the rolled hem width is labeled with an "M.")

4. Change to a fine needle, size 9/60 to 12/80.

5. Thread your serger. Because nylon monofilament is hard to see and woolly stretch nylon is fluffy, tie-on and pull threads through, then use a needle threader or a thread cradle (see page 34 in *Creative Serging Illustrated*) to thread the looper and needle eyes.

6. Adjust the thread tensions so they are unbalanced. Tighten the lower looper to form a straight line on the wrong side. *The upper looper should roll to the wrong side, completely encasing the edge; loosen if necessary.* Needle tension is *normal; loosen if the fabric puckers.*

7. If your serger has a slower speed setting, use it. When starting, *hold the thread chain to prevent jamming.* For better edge rolling, trim off 1/8-1/4". Serge off at the corners. *Rounding the corners slightly will prevent the corners from becoming too pointed;* angle in about 1/8" for the last three or four stitches and start the next edge about 1/8" in, then angle out (Fig. 11-2).

NAPKIN CORNERS: ←ANGLE IN ⅛" & OUT FROM THE CORNER→

Fig. 11-2

☞ **Update tip:** You'll notice that the lengthwise grain rolls the best but has a tendency to pucker. *Eliminate puckers by loosening the needle tension, taut-serging (holding the fabric taut in front and back of the presser foot), and/or shortening the stitch length.* Or, if your serger has differential feed, adjust for taut-sewing, usually at the .7 setting. On the crosswise grain, "pokeys" (fibers that won't roll) can sometimes be a problem. *Eliminate pokeys by widening the stitch, tightening the upper looper tension, or, as a last resort, widening the bite* (consult your manual and see pages 136-137).

For difficult fabrics that won't roll no matter what you do, try woolly stretch nylon in the lower looper, or both loopers, and serge with a balanced tension narrow rolled stitch.

8. When using woolly stretch nylon (in one or both loopers), place a dot of seam sealant on each corner. When dry, trim the excess thread chain. When using nylon monofilament thread (in the loopers and needle), fuse the thread ends by melting. Cut the thread chain to 1/2". Place the chain near, but not in, the blue part of a candle flame. *The thread should melt but not actually burn.* Slowly melt the

Napkins Assume Other Identities

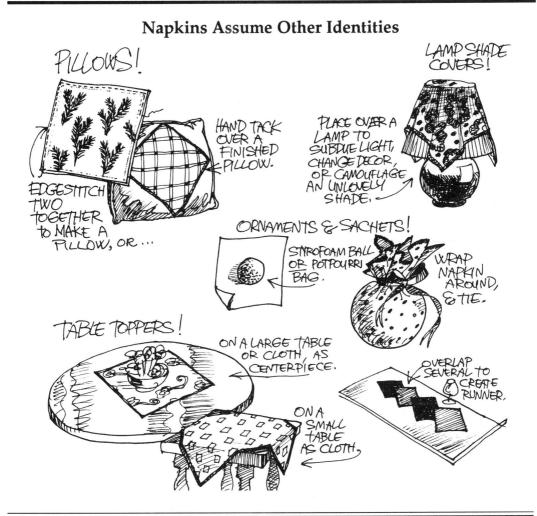

PILLOWS!

EDGESTITCH TWO TOGETHER TO MAKE A PILLOW, OR...

HAND TACK OVER A FINISHED PILLOW.

LAMP SHADE COVERS!

PLACE OVER A LAMP TO SUBDUE LIGHT, CHANGE DECOR, OR CAMOUFLAGE AN UNLOVELY SHADE.

ORNAMENTS & SACHETS!

STYROFOAM BALL OR POTPOURRI BAG.

WRAP NAPKIN AROUND, & TIE.

TABLE TOPPERS!

ON A LARGE TABLE OR CLOTH, AS CENTERPIECE.

ON A SMALL TABLE AS CLOTH,

OVERLAP SEVERAL TO CREATE RUNNER.

thread back to the napkin corner. See Fig. 11-3.

9. Press the napkins. Use a synthetic or low iron setting when pressing napkin edges serged with nylon thread.

☞ *Update tip:* Napkins can assume many identities—as pillow or lamp-shade covers, table toppers, sachets, you name it.

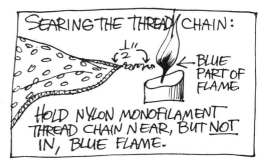

SEARING THE THREAD CHAIN:

BLUE PART OF FLAME

HOLD NYLON MONOFILAMENT THREAD CHAIN NEAR, BUT NOT IN, BLUE FLAME.

Fig. 11-3

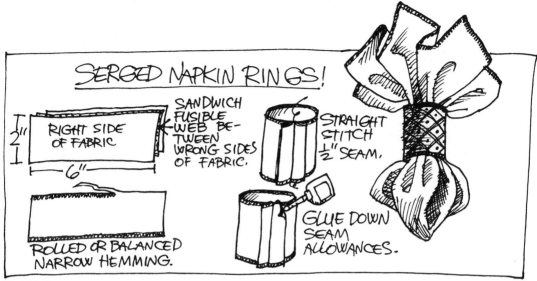

Fig. 11-4

Serged Napkin Rings

Follow these steps to make napkin rings like the one shown in Fig. 11-4).

1. For each ring, cut out two strips of matching or coordinating fabric and one strip of fusible web, all cut about 2" wide by 6" long.

2. Sandwich the fusible web between the wrong sides of two strips. Fuse the strips together.

3. *With the right side up*, finish the two long edges with narrow rolled hem or balanced hemming. Trim each side slightly as you serge.

4. Straight-stitch the short ends right sides together using 1/2" seam allowances. Dab glue stick or craft glue to the underside of the seam allowances, then finger-press open and flat. Allow to dry.

5. Turn the napkin ring right side out.

Never-Miss
Mitered Placemats

Invest one or two hours serging and sewing these mitered placemats, copies of a designer brand sold in the finest linen departments and shops.

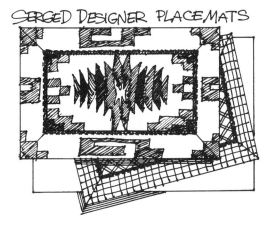

Materials Needed

✎ **Note:** Yardage specifications vary with the number of placemats and are given for quantities of four, six, and eight.

- **Fabric.** For the border—1 yard for four, 1-1/3 yards for six, or 1-7/8 yards for eight. For the inset—1/2 yard for four or 1 yard for six or eight of 45"-wide cotton or cotton blend. (The border and inset colors should contrast.)

- **Nonwoven fusible interfacing.** 2-2/3 yards for four, 4 yards for six, or 3-5/8 yards for eight of 22"-wide, crisp, medium-weight interfacing like Pellon's *ShirTailor*.

- **Fusible transfer web.** 1-1/4 yards for four, 1-7/8 yards for six, or 2-1/2 yards for eight of 18"-wide paper-backed web, like Pellon's *Wonder-Under* or Aleene's *Hot Stitch*™.

- **Thread.** One spool of decorative thread (for the upper looper) to match or contrast with the fabric and two spools or cones (for the lower looper and needle) of serger thread to match or contrast with the decorative thread. Wind two bobbins of the serger thread for use in the top and bobbin of your conventional machine.

Cutting Directions

Use the dimensions shown in Fig. 11-5.

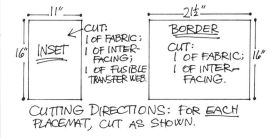

Fig. 11-5

Serger Settings

A narrow width, short, balanced, 3-thread stitch. Adjust the stitch length according to the decorative thread used; the thicker the looper thread used, the longer the stitch required.

Fastest Serging and Sewing Order

1. **Fuse** the interfacing to the wrong sides of the corresponding border and inset pieces.

2. **Fuse** the transfer web to the wrong side of the interfaced insets. Peel away the paper backing.

3. Wrong sides together, **center** the inset on the border, as shown. **Fuse** the inset to the border. See Fig. 11-6.

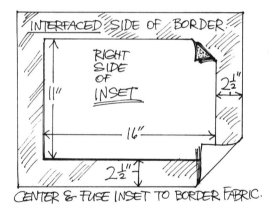

CENTER & FUSE INSET TO BORDER FABRIC.

Fig. 11-6

4. On the right side of the border pieces, **serge-finish** all four placemat sides. (Don't worry about the corner threads—the corners will be mitered.)

5. **Press** 2" hems in all sides of the borders, toward the insets.

6. **Mark** the 2" hemline corner points (where the hemlines intersect) on all the placemats. See Fig. 11-7.

7. **Fold** corners right sides together, aligning the two serged edges (Fig. 11-8).

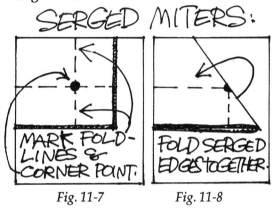

| Fig. 11-7 | Fig. 11-8 |

8. **Fold** the corners again, as shown, aligning all serged edges (Fig. 11-9).

9. Using the fold line as a guide, **straight-stitch** next to (but not catching) the fold. **Backstitch** at the serged edge. See Fig. 11-10.

| Fig. 11-9 | Fig. 11-10 |

10. **Trim** to a 1/4" seam, tapering at the corner point to minimize bulk (Fig. 11-11).

11. **Press** open the trimmed seam. Then **turn** right side out. Center the miter in the border corner and **press** again from the right side. See Fig. 11-12.

Fig. 11-11   Fig. 11-12

12. **Edge-stitch** close to the decorative stitching to secure the border.

Serged Sheet Covers

Take advantage of white sales to serge inexpensive sheet cover-ups for your furniture and windows. The dramatic, family-pleasing results are fast and affordable.

Pattern and publishing companies are right on target, offering progressive, easy-to-sew styles. You'll find how-to's mirroring nearly every soft furnishing trend seen at retail. For ideas, refer to the "Craft" and "Home Decorating" catalog tabs and your fabric store's home decorating books. (Because of large decorating dimensions and wide variability of furniture sizes, most are not actually patterns, but guidesheets or instruction booklets.)

• After pinpointing your project, estimate the number of and size of sheets required. Generally, wide-width sheets will eliminate piecing. Pulling out the hem stitches will also yield more useable fabric. The following are standard sheet sizes, but keep in mind that dimensions vary brand to brand.

Standard flat sheet sizes (after letting out the hems):

Twin: 66" wide by 104" long

Double: 81" wide by 104" long

Queen: 90" wide by 110" long

King: 108" wide by 110" long

Queen is the most versatile sheet size and the easiest to equate to 45"-width yardage requirements; there's a generous six yards in each queen sheet. Some yardage examples: One queen will cover two folding chairs or make a full-length cloth for a 30"-diameter round table and one king is enough for a draped cover on an easy chair. *Decorative borders and must-be-matched motifs decrease the yardage yield* and necessitate buying more sheets.

• After the sheet has been fit and cut to the correct dimensions, simply hem or edge-finish. **Decorative double-finishing** is a combination technique that adds body and stitching accents to hems and edges. It's Gail's preference for hemming continuously curved edges, like rounded tablecloth or furniture throw hems. Allow a 1/2" hem. With decorative thread (like pearl cotton or rayon) in the upper looper and *the wrong side up,* serge-

finish the edge, trimming off 1/8-1/4". Turn to the right side, as shown, and edge-stitch with matching thread. (If using a printed sheet, turn a narrower hem to the right side, so that the wrong side doesn't show.) Press. See Fig. 11-13.

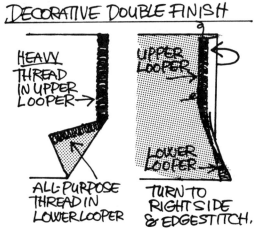

DECORATIVE DOUBLE FINISH

HEAVY THREAD IN UPPER LOOPER→

ALL-PURPOSE THREAD IN LOWER LOOPER

UPPER LOOPER→

LOWER LOOPER→

TURN TO RIGHT SIDE & EDGESTITCH.

Fig. 11-13

The flatlocked double hem is a serge-only technique that is perfect for straight ruffles, curtains, square and rectangular tablecloths, and furniture throws. The double-layer hem discourages billowing. Allow a 2-6" hem. Turn half the hem allowance up to the hemline on the wrong side. Press.

Turn up half the hem allowance again to the wrong side; the second fold is the hemline. Press. Turn up the same amount again to the wrong side. Flatlock along the third fold, *letting the stitches hang over the edge*, and pull flat (the loops of the upper looper, not the ladder of the lower looper, will be on the right side). Decorative thread in the upper looper is optional. See Fig. 11-14.

FLATLOCKED DOUBLE HEM

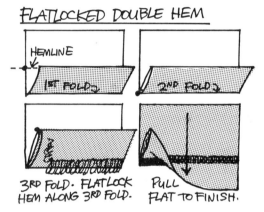

Fig. 11-14

• When making soft throws for furniture, covering the cushions separately will secure the throw and create a neater, more fitted design. **These fast cushion covers** save time, sheets, and money by covering only the part of the cushion that shows—primarily the top and sides. Contour the sheet to the cushion, adding at least 4" extra to the side depth for the underside extension. Pin out the fullness at the corners, straight-stitch the darts, and try the cover on the cushion again. Fit should be tight for the most professional look.

After the fit has been confirmed and the darts backstitched, serge-finish and trim, as shown in Fig. 11-15. To draw

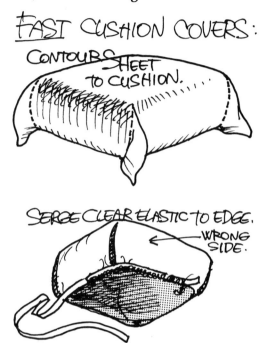

Fig. 11-15

in the cushion, serge 3/8"-width polyurethane elastic to the wrong side of the raw edge. *Stretch the elastic vigorously within 4" of each corner and slightly along the sides.* The edge will cup in in a way that's similar to the cupped edges of a fitted sheet. Put the cover on the cushion, right side out. *Optional:* For complete coverage, hand-tack a sheet piece (cut to cushion bottom size) to the underside before putting on the cover.

Update tip: Using the fast cushion cover methods, you can serge flat sheets into fitted sheets (Fig. 11-16).

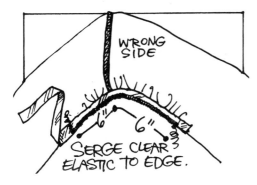

Fig. 11-16

• Utilize **seams-out serging**. To eliminate a step when making curtains (see "Instant Draped Curtains" and "Circle Curtains," pages 127-129), swags and tie-backs, simply place the fabrics wrong sides together and serge-seam together. (No more tedious turning right sides out.) A narrow rolled or balanced stitch is worthy of this exposure; it covers the edge well, while adding a subtle but decorative stitching line. See Fig. 11-17.

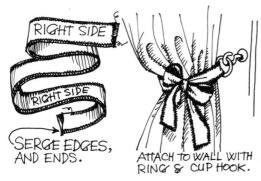

Fig. 11-17

• To gather **long ruffle strips,** serge over *(but not through)* heavy thread, secure one end, and pull the other.

• Create **custom-serged piping accents.** For more details on serged piping, see pages 52-56.

Sources: For polyurethane elastic, shop your local fabric store or these mail-order suppliers: Clotilde, Nancy's Notions, Serge and Sew Notions, and Stretch & Sew Fabrics (see "Serge-by-Mail Directory," pages 162-173).

Serger-Strip Patchwork and Quilting

If your great-grandmother had owned a serger, her quilts would have been serged together. Now, any quilt design that can be strip-pieced can be easily serged. Simply combine basic serger principles with your favorite strip-piecing techniques to create pieced quilting designs quickly, yet accurately. We call this new method "serger-strip patchwork."

Strip-Pieced Quilt

Eleanor Burns, strip-piecing special-ist and author of numerous *Quilt in a Day* books, states, "With the use of the overlock, rotary cutter, and a 6" by 24" ruler, I had the (quilt) top pieced in a short five hours." Serge a Log Cabin, Amish Shadow, Irish Chain, or any other strip-piecing design using these basic guidelines:

• **Serge a test seam** on a scrap prior to cutting the strips for a quilt top. Check the seam strength and measure the seam width. Experience has shown that a wide seam width and a shorter-than-normal stitch length will produce the most secure piecing seam. (In fact, if your machine has 3/4-thread capa-bility, use that durable stitch.)

✎ **Note:** Serged seam width can be as wide as 3/8". If so, cut the quilt strips slightly wider, allowing for a 3/8" seam allowance, instead of the stan-dard 1/4".

• For speed and efficiency, **rotary-cut the fabric strips** (Fig. 11-18). You can cut many layers of the same fabric at once if the blade is sharp.

ROTARY-CUT FABRIC STRIPS.

Fig. 11-18

• **Serge-seam the strips together.** Allow the serger blades to barely trim off the fabric whiskers, not the seam allowance width. After serging, press the seams flat and then press to one side. Using a serger will speed up the quilt piecing process and, with the serger's extended feed dog system, will more evenly feed the strips together. See Fig. 11-19.

SERGE-SEAM FABRIC STRIPS.

Fig. 11-19

- **Rotary-cut the strips into patchwork** strips, realign, and rotary-cut again (if this applies to your design). See Figs. 11-20 and 11-21.

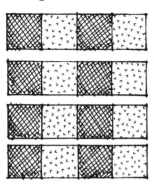

ROTARY-CUT INTO PATCH-WORK STRIPS.

Fig. 11-20

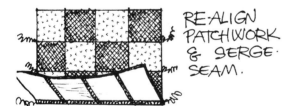

RE-ALIGN PATCHWORK & SERGE-SEAM.

Fig. 11-21

- After piecing the quilt top with serging, **machine-quilt, hand-tie, or hand-quilt** the quilt top to the batting and backing fabrics.

☞ **Update tip:** For fast furnishing accents, use serger-strip patchwork cut on the bias (Fig. 11-22). Bias patch-

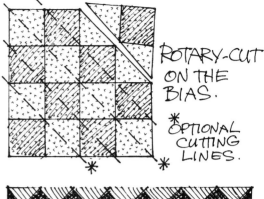

ROTARY-CUT ON THE BIAS.

* OPTIONAL CUTTING LINES.

USE BIAS PATCHWORK FOR BINDINGS, PIPING, DECORATIVE INSERTS.

Fig. 11-22

work is perfect for bindings, piping, and decorative inserts. Or, integrate narrow bias patchwork in other serged-piecing designs (Fig. 11-23).

OR USE NARROW BIAS PATCH-WORK STRIPS IN OTHER DESIGNS – SERGE-SEAM STRIPS (NON-BIAS) TOGETHER.

Fig. 11-23

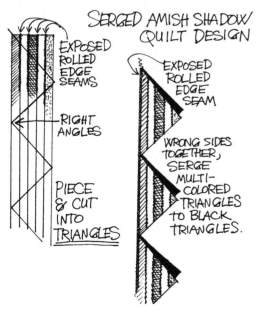

Exposed Patchwork Seams

For a contemporary angle on serger-strip patchwork, expose the seams. A narrow stitch width (preferably rolled) with a short stitch length seam looks best. Choose a decorative thread like a cotton or rayon machine-embroidery thread for the upper looper. *Serge with wrong sides together.* See Fig. 11-24.

Fig. 11-24

Try using this exposed rolled-edge technique on an Amish Shadow design. For traditional color combinations, cut 1" strips of five brilliant colors. Serge all five strips together using a different thread color at each seam. Or, for dramatic contrast, use black decorative thread throughout. Press all rolled-edge seams to one side so the decorative right side of the seam is visible.

☞ **Update tip:** If you'd rather not change thread colors with each seam, use clear monofilament nylon thread in the needle and lower looper; it will "disappear," blending with all the colors.

Use a gridded template or ruler and cut right-angle triangles from serged strips (Fig. 11-24). Use the same template to cut identical triangles from black fabric. Continuously serge multicolored strips to the dark fabric to form blocks. Serge the blocks together in the design of your choice (Fig. 11-25).

Fig. 11-25

Reversible Serger-Strip Quilting

Reversible strip quilting is a speed quilting technique that was designed with serger owners in mind. Kaye Wood, author of *Serger Patchwork Projects*, serges the backing, batting, and top fabric at the same time to create durable and reversible quilt projects.

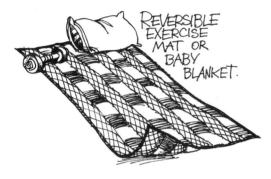

For a first project, serge an exercise mat or baby blanket.

1. Cut 16 strips of fabric, each 4" by 45". Also cut eight 4" by 45" strips of polyester fleece or batting.

2. Make a quilt sandwich by placing a strip of fabric on each side of a batting strip. *Place the wrong sides of the fabric to the batting.* Serge both long edges with a medium-width and medium-length overlock stitch; the first quilt sandwich has been formed. See Fig. 11-26.

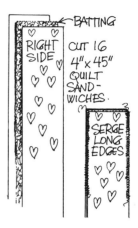

Fig. 11-26

3. On both sides of this quilt sandwich, place a fabric strip, right sides together. Pin all layers together along one long edge. Place a batting strip on the underside. Adjust the serger for the widest overlock seam width and a medium-length stitch. *Serge all layers together with the batting next to the feed dogs. See Fig. 11-27. It will be necessary to widen and lengthen the overlock stitch to serge through ALL the layers.*

Fig. 11-27

4. Fold the fabric strips so right sides are visible, covering the batting. Serge the raw edges of this second quilt sandwich. Repeat these steps until all eight quilt sandwiches have been added. Decoratively serge-finish or bind the edges of the finished quilt. See Fig. 11-28.

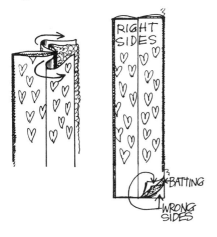

Fig. 11-28

Instant Draped Curtains

Draping is nearly a no-sew method. For window or shower curtains, drape the fabric over the curtain rod. When you've got gobs of fabric, and no time to spare, this method's the ticket.

1. **Cut the fabric length 2 to 2-1/2 times the length desired** (Fig. 11-29). (Draped folds are soft and lavish when there's twice the length of fabric to hang behind, weight and self-line the front layer.)

2. **Serge-finish the shorter, crosswise ends** (Fig. 11-29). *Optional:* shorter than full-length or floor-length swags can be serge-finished at a 45-degree

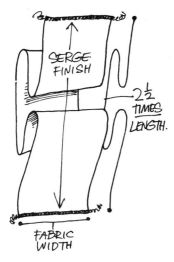

Fig. 11-29

angle. The swag hem on each side will be shorter in the front, angled down to the back.

3. **Place the fabric over the rod to create the curtain.** Any excess length can fall on the floor in an unhemmed puddle (the latest decorating craze and the epitome of casual elegance). For tie-backs, see page 122.

Circle Curtains

This ingenious curtain style is self-lined, so the fullness drapes beautifully. Actually a large casing through which the curtain rod is inserted, the curtain can be rotated to even fading. Because circle curtains look terrific from the other side of the window, try them as room dividers or shower curtains too.

1. **Choose light- to medium-weight fabric.** Avoid one-way naps or prints. To calculate yardage, multiply two to three times the window width by twice the length desired plus 4". The lengthwise grain runs parallel to the window height.

☞ **Update tip:** Instead of piecing for the width required, just make the number of curtain casings required. The unseamed edges are hidden in the curtain fullness and the casings can be divided as the climate, view, and privacy demand.

2. **Cut the fabric yardage into the lengths needed;** each length should be twice the desired curtain length plus 4".

3. If necessary, **serge-finish the lengthwise edges** (a narrow rolled stitch is optional); otherwise, the selvage edge finish will suffice. See Fig. 11-30.

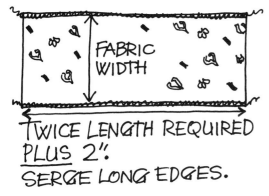

TWICE LENGTH REQUIRED PLUS 2". SERGE LONG EDGES.

Fig. 11-30

4. Fold each length in half, right sides together, and **serge-seam the shorter crosswise ends.** Turn right side out— the curtain is finished. See Fig. 11-31.

FABRIC WITH WRONG SIDE OUT.

SERGE SEAM.

FINISHED CURTAIN— SEVERAL MAY BE NEEDED FOR A WIDE WINDOW.

Fig. 11-31

Thread the rod through the casing(s), arranging the fullness for even distribution. If the seamline is conspicuous, position it at the top edge or bottom hem of the casing. Tie backs are optional (see page 122).

EASY TIE-BACKS

☞ **Update tip:** Run weighted tape or chain, available in upholstery supply departments and stores, along the inside of the bottom hem fold for added weight. The curtain will be less billowy, the fullness more uniform.

Quick Cord Cover-ups

Have lamp or TV cords that clash with your decor? Cover them with fabric—it's fast and safe. It's also stunning when coordinated to swag lampshades.

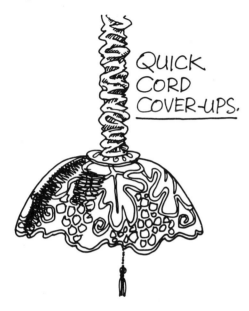

1. Cut a strip of light- to medium-weight smooth-textured fabric, twice the length of the cord by 4" wide (wide enough so that when folded in half lengthwise the cover will fit over the plug).

2. Serge-seam to piece the strip length as necessary. Then fold the strip in half, lengthwise, wrong sides together. With a narrow rolled or balanced stitch, serge-seam the raw edges together. See Fig. 11-32.

Fig. 11-32

3. Slip the cover over the plug, onto the cord, shirring the fullness evenly (Fig. 11-33).

Fig. 11-33

Serged Decorations: Replace Paper With Fabric

Because of the fast-finished, flat edges, serged fabric can be substituted for paper materials in holiday decorations—looped garlands, bows, ribbons, even gift wrap. Daring enough to break paper traditions? You'll be rewarded by the incomparable color depth, season-after-season durability, recyclability, and drapability unique to fabric crafts. Most are kid-proof and pet-proof, too; after serging, let the whole family join the fabricating fun.

• Recollect cutting and pasting paper strips into paper chain loop **garlands**? Retain the clever looping concept, but upgrade the materials: replace the construction paper with holiday fabric, the messy paste with tacky craft glue.

1. **Sandwich fusible web** between the wrong sides of two coordinating or contrasting holiday prints or solids. One yard of fabric will yield a 6-yard-long looped garland. **Fuse,** following the package instructions and aligning the selvages. See Fig. 11-34.

Fig. 11-34

2. **Adjust your serger for narrow balanced-tension hemming.** Shorten or lengthen the stitch for adequate edge coverage. Decorative thread in the upper looper is optional.

3. **Serge-finish and cut-out the loop strips at the same time.** Serge parallel to the lengthwise grain for the cleanest, fastest finishing. See Fig. 11-35. Loop

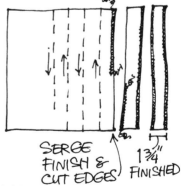

Fig. 11-35

strips should be about 1 3/4" wide, finished. Reverse serging directions, as shown in the next column, so that the stitch will be uniform side-to-side.

4. With sharp scissors, cut the chain loop strips into 7" lengths. **Loop the strips, lap 3/8", and glue.** See Fig. 11-36.

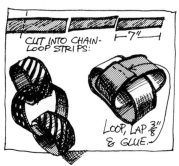

Fig. 11-36

Variations: Narrow, widen, lengthen, or shorten the loop strip to create different sizes and looks; combine different sizes in one garland. Or, alternate the fabrics on the outside, loop-by-loop or in color-blocks.

• Have you priced paper and fabric ribbon lately? Selling for as much as $2.50/yard, you're better off serging your own ribbon and bows. This serge-finished **fabric ribbon** lasts longer, ties softer, and unifies the other tree-trimmings.

1. **Place two holiday solids or prints wrong sides together,** aligning the selvages. (Buy at least a yard of each fabric to yield 12 to 20 one-yard ribbon strips. For package wrappings, buy at least two yards of each fabric to yield longer, more versatile ribbon strips.)

Variations: For stiffer bows, fuse the fabrics together, as described for the looped chain garland. Also, vary the ribbon width.

2. **Adjust your serger for narrow rolled or balanced-tension edge hemming.** Shorten or lengthen the stitch for adequate edge coverage. Decorative thread in the upper looper is optional.

3. **Serge-finish and cut-out the ribbon strips at the same time.** Serge parallel to the lengthwise grain for the cleanest, fastest finishing. Ribbon strips should be 2-3" wide, finished. Reverse serging directions, as shown, so that the stitch will be uniform side-to-side. Angle the

ribbon ends when serge-finishing. See Fig.11-37.

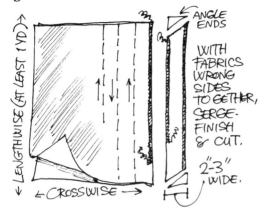

Fig. 11-37

4. Tie the ribbon into tree bows (the one-yard length is ample for a lush bow). Or, use as wreath and package embellishments.

• **Serge a layered tree skirt,** fast. (Also see illustration on page 131.)

1. **Cut two circles** out of 44"-wide (or wider) prequilted or felted fabric or medium-weight woven. For the larger circle, you'll need 1-1/4 yard; cut out a 45" circle. For the smaller circle, you'll need 1 yard; cut out a 35" circle. Pivot a cord or measuring tape from the center of the fabric for accurate marking and cutting of the circle.

2. **Cut each circle to its center point.** Then cut out 8" centers in each (or a center hole to fit your stand).

3. **Adjust your serger for a wide, long balanced tension stitch.** Select a decorative thread, yarn, or ribbon. Test decorative serging on fabric scraps before serging the circle edges.

4. Starting at an inside circle corner (the least conspicuous), **serge-finish the edges of one of the circles.** Repeat for the other size. See Fig. 11-38.

5. **Layer the circles under the tree,** so that the larger circle forms an even border under the smaller circle.

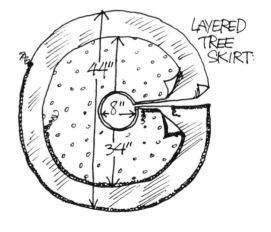

Fig. 11-38

12. Making the Most of Your Serger

When attending sewing shows and seminars, two comments we often hear are: "I've been using my serger for seaming, but I haven't tried the narrow rolled hem yet," and "I have trouble adjusting the stitch, so I haven't been serging."

It's a shame that sergers aren't more fully utilized or even used at all. Learning just a few tips and techniques can get you started toward more, better, and less-frustrating serging. Of course, the best learning center is the dealer where you bought your serger. Ask about classes, videos, and solutions to persistent problems. For a machine-side reference, use this chapter. These tips and enhancements we've collected are taught by some of the best machine technicians around and have made a noticeable difference in the quality of our own serging.

Simple Steps to Improving Stitch Quality

If stitching quality is poor or stitches aren't forming at all, follow these three troubleshooting steps:

1. If the stitch will not adjust to the quality or consistency desired, **try changing the needle first.** A dull, bent, burred, incorrect, or poorly positioned needle is the most common cause of imperfect stitches and the easiest to remedy. See Figs. 12-1 and 12-2.

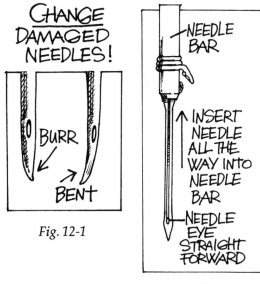

Fig. 12-1

Fig. 12-2

2. **Next, change the thread.** Quality, thickness, pliability, and degree of twist all contribute to stitch characteristics.

☞ **Update tip:** As you experiment with different types of threads, make sample swatches of each, noting the type, brand, and tension settings. For comparison, try each thread on a variety of fabrics.

Thread for serging must be uniform, without slubs; variances in thickness require different tension adjustments, so the stitch will be inconsistent in quality (Fig. 12-3). Also, the thread

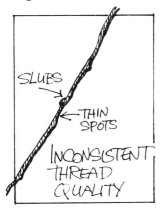

Fig. 12-3

thickness should correspond to the fabric thickness; using a thread that's too heavy on a blouse-weight silk will produce stitches too conspicuous in weight and texture. Instead, use an extra-fine embroidery or lingerie thread. See Fig. 12-4.

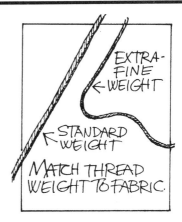

Fig. 12-4

Pliability significantly contributes to stitching success—more than most newcomers to serging realize. *The looper thread must be able to bend*, forming a loop around the needle thread. If the thread doesn't loop, the stitch won't form or will form only intermittently.

Because a serger sews nearly twice as fast as a conventional machine, thread strength is also important. *The thread must withstand the tension and speed, yet not be so strong that it weakens the fabric.* For instance, using all-purpose 100% polyester thread for a narrow rolled edge on taffeta can result in a stitch that tears away from the fabric edge. Nontwisted thread, like woolly stretch nylon, is the better alternative for finishing lighter weight or delicate fabrics; the lack of twist softens the strong nylon fiber and fills in the spaces between stitches for beautiful satin finishing.

3. Finally, **check the positioning of the cutting blades.** Changing or repositioning the blades takes practice, but it is a valuable skill worth the learning time invested.

Know your two blades. These blades work together as the cutting assembly. During serging, one blade unmistakably moves, while the other remains fixed in place; butted together, the two blades cut the fabric edge. See Fig. 12-5. These blades must be aligned

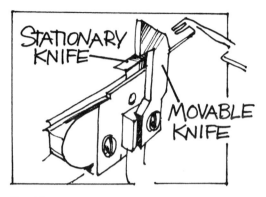

Fig. 12-5

with the right side edge of the stitch finger. (For better understanding of this alignment, take a close look at your serger.)

The width of the serged stitch is determined by the width of the stitch finger. If the cutting width, called the bite, is too narrow, loops will hang over the fabric edge even though the tensions are repeatedly tightened (Fig.

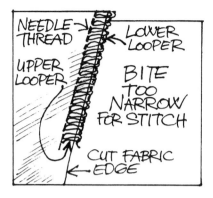

Fig. 12-6

12-6). The same problem of excess loops can occur when sewing stretchy knits; the foot pressure and the cutting action stretches and narrows the knit slightly, causing the threads to extend beyond the edge.

To solve both these excess loop problems, the bite is widened by changing the position of the fixed cutter. See Fig. 12-7.

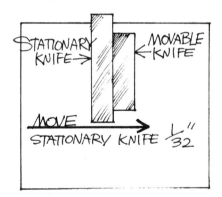

Fig. 12-7

Consult your manual and see the step-by-step tips, below. Move the fixed cutter or knife about 1/32" to the right. If the bite width was changed for serging knits, be sure to adjust back to the original position for serging wovens.

✎ **Note:** If you are hesitant to attempt moving or changing the cutting assembly, but have diagnosed a bite-width problem, ask your favorite dealer for assistance.

To move the cutting assembly, safely:

1. Switch off the serger power or unplug the machine.

2. Remove or push aside the movable knife. Some knives require loosening a screw. Using a long-handled screwdriver will increase your turning and retightening strength. Don't forget: "Righty tighty, lefty loosey."

3. **Loosen or adjust the stationary knife to the right (or left) as necessary.** See Fig. 12-7.

4. Return the movable knife to position. *The two knives must be flush against each other or the assembly will not cut.*

5. Slowly and carefully test-serge on a fabric scrap.

6. Readjust as necessary. If the stitch is looping over the edge, move the fixed cutter to the right. If the fabric edge is being pulled in too much by the stitch, move the fixed cutter to the left. *Remember, you should be moving the cutter in very small (1/32") increments*, testing, then readjusting.

☞ **Update tip:** "Pokeys," fabric threads that persistently poke through stitching, can be cured by the same

Fig. 12-8

bite-widening treatment. See Fig. 12-8. When the bite is wider, more fabric is turned under, over the stitch finger, minimizing raveling. *Caution:* Don't confuse pokeys with a chronically ragged cut edge, indicative of a dull cutter. Generally only the movable (and less expensive) cutter will need replacing.

Serger Troubleshooting with Sue Green

There's not a serger problem Sue Green's afraid to tackle and she's never met a machine she didn't like (well, almost never). Coincidentally, she is the author of *Know Your Serger*, a troubleshooting guide for all brands and models, and she is coauthor of *Creative Serging Illustrated* (see "References," page 174).

Fabric Jams

Ever accidentally try to serge a 5/8" seam with the knives disengaged? Jamming of the fabric occurs. The untrimmed fabric rolls over and gets tangled in the stitches and loopers. Although there is a safe way to remove the fabric without damaging it, let this regrettable situation be a reminder: *If the knives are disengaged, the fabric should not extend beyond the right side of the needle plate.*

To safely remove the jammed fabric (see Fig. 12-9):

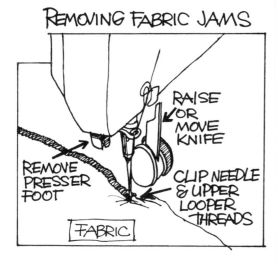

Fig. 12-9

1. Remove the serger presser foot.

2. Clip the needle thread(s) close to the stitches.

3. Clip the upper looper thread strand as close to the fabric as possible.

4. Pull slack in the lower looper thread below the tension dial.

5. Gently remove the fabric from the stitch finger by pulling to the back of the machine until it is released.

6. Remove the stitches from the fabric.

7. Rethread the needle(s) and upper looper.

Threads That Break After Rethreading

Have you experienced this problem before? *After rethreading, the lower looper thread breaks, requiring more tedious rethreading.* To rethread the lower looper, you turned the handwheel until the lower looper was in its far left position. Then, you threaded the left eye or hook and turned the handwheel until the eye in the tip of the looper was exposed on the right. Finally, you threaded the right eye. But when you serged again, the thread broke again. Why?

The movement of the lower looper from the left position to the right caused the looper to pick up the needle thread(s) as it passed across; a stitch started to form before the last eye in the looper was threaded. The needle thread(s) were wrapped around the looper and trapped. *When you began to serge, the threads crossed each other and the one with the greatest stress—normally the lower looper—broke again.* See Fig. 12-10.

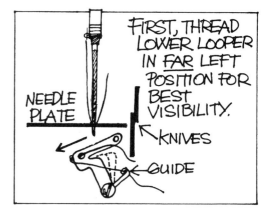

Fig. 12-10

To position the threads correctly after rethreading the lower looper, pull the needle threads out of the needleplate before stitching again. Raise the needle to the highest position and use your tweezers to draw the thread out. See Fig. 12-11.

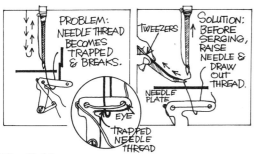

Fig. 12-11

☞ **Update tip:** Some serger owners find this alternative solution ingenious and easy to remember: Unthread the needle(s), rethread the lower looper, and then rethread the needle(s).

Neat Feet

Feet are a hot item in the serger world, and companies are continually introducing new feet with expanded capabilities. Call your local dealer occasionally for an update on what is available. Keep in mind that brands can sometimes be mixed (the Baby Lock blind-hem foot, for instance, will fit many Singer overlocks). Some feet come as standard equipment with the initial serger purchase. Others are optional. Understanding their intended use and creative capabilities will speed and improve your serging.

- **All-purpose feet,** sold with the serger, may be used when overlocking a variety of widths. (Some brands, however, require a foot change to achieve a narrow rolled or balanced stitch.) The foot may have one or more guides or guide holes. These allow a stabilizer like heavy thread (for gathering) or stay tape (to prevent stretching) to be serged over uniformly, without hand manipulation.

- Some serger brands or models also have **snap-off feet.** A shank remains in place, held with a screw, while the working bases can be removed and exchanged. Another variation on the all-purpose foot is the ability to swing out the foot for unencumbered access when threading and needle changing.

- **Blind-hem feet** are available for most serger brands. Preparation for a serged blind hem is the same as marking and folding for a conventionally sewn blind hem. The blind-hem foot has a metal guide that sits against the fold and ensures a consistent needle bite (Fig. 12-12). Some feet are adjust-

Fig. 12-12

able, while others come in a range of sizes for different fabric thicknesses. A serged blind hem shows least on spongy knits or outerwear such as sweatshirting or polyfleece; the stitch bite is easily pressed or pulled out, and the thread is hidden in the texture. Except for heavily textured fabrics, a serged blind stitch is too conspicuous on wovens.

☞ **Update tip:** Try using the blind-hem foot anytime serging without cutting is required (such as flatlocking or flatlocked topstitching).

• **Elastic guide feet,** also called *elasticators* or *elastic applicators,* hold the elastic strip in place under the foot so it can be serged flat without pinning. The adjusting screw regulates the amount of tension on the elastic. See Fig. 12-13.

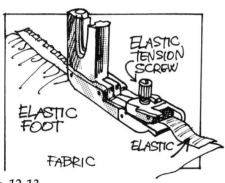

Fig. 12-13

To establish the ratio, remove the needle thread and feed in a 12" strip of elastic marked every 3". Just as one of the marks goes under the foot, put in a 6" piece of fabric. (This simulates the 2:1 ratio used in many activewear patterns.) The next mark and the edge of the fabric should match. If not,

adjust the screw (right for more stretching, left for less) and repeat until they do.

• **Piping feet** are grooved to accommodate piping when serging it to a single layer or sandwiching it between two layers (Fig. 12-14). The groove is

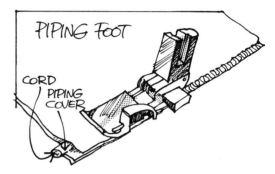

Fig. 12-14

on the bottom of the foot, to the left of the needle line (Fig. 12-15). (Refer to

Fig. 12-15

"Serged Piping," on page 52.) It's also handy for inserting zippers (see "Serged Zipper Applications," pages 7-9). These feet are not available from every manufacturer or for every model.

• **Bead strand applicators** allow smooth feeding of a fine bead strand through the channels under the back and over the front of the foot (Fig. 12-16), directly between the needle and

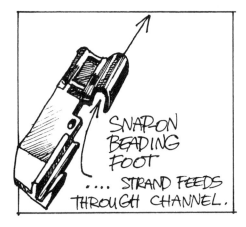

Fig. 12-16

the cutter. (For more details, see "Serging Bead Strands," page 63.) Also, bead applicators are handy for serging over purchased cording or heavy yarns.

• **Tape guide feet** are new to the serger market and are currently being sold only by Elna, Inc., for some (not all) of their ElnaLock models (other companies may develop their own versions, so be on the lookout). "Tape guide" is a bit of a misnomer the foot facilitates folding and serging of a tape strip between two layers of fabric to

create a pipinglike seam insertion. See Fig. 12-17. Elna's literature smartly suggests the timesaving strategy of cutting your own tape strips with the serger (remove the needles first).

Fig. 12-17

• **Bias binder feet** have also been introduced by Elna, Inc., for their Elna-Lock models with double-chainstitch capability. Like the tape guide, the bias binder foot folds flat strips (about 1-3/8" wide) around the edge (to a finished width of about 3/8"). See Fig. 12-18. But the binding is chainstitched,

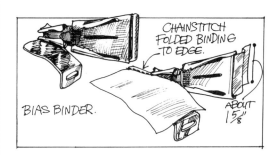

Fig. 12-18

rather than overlocked, into place. The bound edge replicates bindings seen on ready-made T-shirts, sportswear, and decorating accessories. Again, consider stripping binding fabric with your serger.

Sources: Check with your dealer first. (By the time you read this, there may be new feet, or feet comparable to those mentioned above, available for your serger.) For mail order, try Sewing Emporium and The Sewing Place (see addresses in "Serge-by-Mail Directory," page 167).

Hot Serger Hints

Here are the latest, best hints learned since the writing of *Creative Serging Illustrated*.

Easier Threading

• Fold 1"-2" of thread back on itself and twist. The thread is stiffer and easier to push through guides and eyes. See Fig. 12-19.

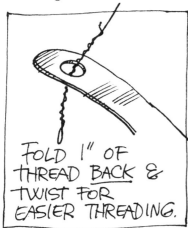

Fig. 12-19

• Wax thread tails with beeswax to eliminate the need for tweezers when threading.

Stitching Accuracy

• When determining stitch width, a good guideline is a wider stitch for heavier fabrics, a narrower stitch for lighter weight fabrics.

• *Watch the front of the foot, not the needle area*, to serge accurately (Fig. 12-20). (By the time the fabric reaches the

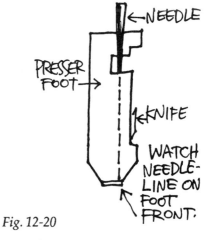

Fig. 12-20

needle, it has already been cut, so at that point it's too late to change the position anyway.) On most standard serger feet the cutting position is marked on the front of the foot; if not, mark it carefully with a fine, permanent marker. Also, mark the needle-line(s) if the manufacturer hasn't already done so.

- For gauging seam widths, use a stick-on seam-width guide (Fig. 12-21). Position it on the front looper cover and stick on. (Available at retail stores and through mail-order notions companies.)

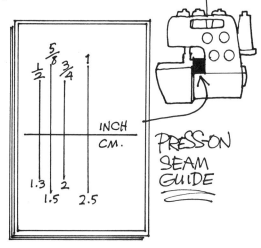

Fig. 12-21

New Needle Options

- The problem of needle-cutting on serged interlock knits can be solved. When holes appear along the seamline, the cause is one or more of the following reasons: the needle is too large, the stitches are too short, or the thread is too large. Test for each possibility to solve the problem. If your machine uses household needles, change to a universal or ball point.

✎ **Note:** Ball point industrial serger needles are now available. Ask your dealer or contact mail-order firms like Nancy's Notions or Sewing Emporium. (For addresses, see "Serge-by-Mail Directory," pages 163-173.)

Jam-proofing

- After serging, chain off at least 2" to avoid the thread chain flipping back and catching in the stitching. Also, the 2" chain can be held when starting to serge again.

- Hold the thread chain (which should be under the back of the foot) and start slowly. Also, pretrim bulky seam intersections.

Solution to a Problem We Hope You Never Have

- If you or your little ones accidentally "oil" your serger with seam sealant (like *Fray Check*™ or *No-Fray*™), take it to a dealer immediately. Be sure to tell your dealer exactly where the sealant was put, because that will make a difference in the cleaning procedure. If your dealer is not familiar with the cleaning solvent needed, the manufacturer recommends rubbing alcohol. To prevent a future mishap, store oil and seam sealant bottles separately and out of the children's reach.

Cleaning without Forced Air

- If you are concerned about chlorofluorocarbon in canned air products (this ingredient can contribute to reduction of ozone in the upper atmosphere), look for those specifically ozone-safe, such as *TAC Air Blast*. It was brought to our attention by Clotilde Lampe, of Clotilde mail-order notions company.

Or, clean your serger instead with a small, hard-bristled artist's paintbrush. The brush will easily pick up most lint if it is first lightly coated with regular sewing machine oil. These brushes can be found in any art supply store.

Also, hand-held computer vacuums can suck up lots of the potentially problem-causing lint and cuttings. Look for them at office supply or computer stores. One we've seen advertised is the *System Sweeper*, an AC-powered mini-vacuum with special attachments designed to reach tiny, hard-to-clean areas. (Available from MicroComputer Accessories, Inc., 5405 Jandy Place, P.O. Box 66911, Los Angeles, CA 90066, 800/521-5270.)

Serger Smarts: Tips from the Sergeon

Bruce Finfrock, who lives and works in Mt. Vernon, Washington, grew up in the serger business and has been servicing sergers since 1975. Among friends, he calls himself the "Serger Sergeon." (Actually he's a serger sales-person and repair specialist at Boomer's Sewing and Vacuum Center, Mt. Vernon, Washington.) We asked Bruce to summarize how we can all make the most of our machines:

• **People should at least read their manuals and take classes,** if they're offered. You should leave the store knowing how to thread the serger, adjust tensions, replace the needles, and disengage the knife.

• **Make sure you have a supply of the right size and type needles** for your machine. It is my opinion that the size 11 needles that are shipped from Japan with the sergers are too fine for the coned and all-purpose threads used in the United States and Canada. For most, I change to a size 12 or 14, to accommodate the relatively thicker thread. The thread must be able to hide in the long groove in the front of the needle.

✎ **Note:** See "Buying the Right Serger Needles," pages 152-153.

• **Use tweezers to insert the needles properly.** Hold the needle in position with the tweezers—push it all the way up. The needle eye should face directly front. With the other hand, set the screw with a screwdriver.

• For better leverage, **use a long-handled screwdriver,** not the one that comes in your machine accessory box. Adjusting the bite width by moving the knife requires a stout grip. You simply have more power with those screwdrivers 8" or longer.

• **Don't blame your machine's timing until threading, tensions, and needles are thoroughly checked out.** Timing is how the machine components work together, and when— the needles, loopers, feed dogs, and so on. Each brand has timing gauges that we use to measure the different components, such as needle height. I adjust some brands more than others for timing problems.

• **If you'd like a shorter stitch length, talk to your dealer.** Stitch length can generally be shortened some. However, the range remains the same, so an equivalent increment will be lost at the end of the longer stitches. But, for those who want a shorter stitch, this is seldom a problem.

• **Take your serger in for servicing at least once a year,** particularly during the first two years. For cottage industry use, twice a year would be recommended. At most dealers, basic servicing runs between $29 and $50 (as of 1989). For that, the mechanic should go through the entire machine, clean and recalibrate it, oil it, grease the gears, and so on.

• **Understand that routine servicing is not covered in the warranty** and will be paid for separately unless the customer has a special arrangement with the dealer. Standard serger warranties are limited, not full. Before buying a serger, the warranty should be thoroughly discussed with the dealer to alleviate any misunderstandings later. Most sergers are covered by the warranty for manufacturer's defects, not normal wear and tear on the machine. For example, if you try to pull fabric out of your serger and in the process, the looper gets broken, the repair is not covered by the warranty.

13. Machine Update: A Guide to Smart Serger Shopping

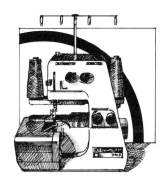

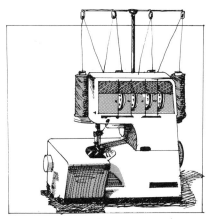

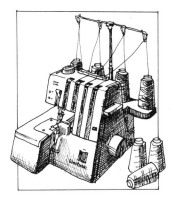

Serging's here to stay, winning over even die-hard lockstitch purists. Why? Serging offers significantly faster sewing and professional looks, without sacrificing construction quality. Rather than *"Should I buy?"* the widespread question currently asked by enthusiasts ready to upgrade and home sewers not yet serging is *"Which one?"* (Fig. 13-1).

Whether you're contemplating buying your first serger, upgrading, or adding to your collection, arriving at an answer to "Which one?" calls for comparing and testing. Start sorting out the variations in brands, models, and features by reading this chapter. From the brief descriptions here, you'll be better able to determine which new features will enhance your brand of sewing.

✎ **Note:** If you've got the time, write to all the serger companies (see "Serger Companies," page 162) before shopping. Ask for dealer referrals and information on all their latest models. You'll receive lots of useful, intriguing information: color brochures, comparison charts, and names of dealers in your area. Bone up and jot down a few questions to ask when shopping and test-serging.

Fig. 13-1

After you've got a grasp of the features and terminology, visit every serger dealer in your area. *There's no question about it—your best source for in-depth information is a reliable dealer.* Conscientious retailers will encourage you to test-serge and thread any prospective model. After test-serging several, narrow your choices down to your favorite models and a dealer who can be depended on for ongoing information, classes, repairs, and parts.

Features: Key Questions and Considerations

Number of Threads

The more threads the better? Perhaps, but not necessarily. More mean more stitch capabilities but also more threading and thread. Also, compare stitch capabilities (see below) as well as threads. (After studying the market, you'll note that there are different types of 4-thread stitches; for instance, a 3/4 safety stitch and a 4/2-thread chainstitch/overedge combination. See the "Glossary of Stitches," pages 157-158.) *The number of thread cones or spools required equals the number in the stitch description.* Hence, four cones or spools are necessary for serging a 4-thread safety stitch overlock or a 4-thread chainstitch/overedge, whereas only two are necessary for 2-thread overedging.

Needles

Industry insiders still argue about the virtues of industrial needles *("more durable and reliable")* versus household needles *("less costly and more readily available in a variety of sizes")*. It's up to you, but don't base your serger selection on needle preference alone. Also see "Buying the Right Serger Needle," page 152.

Stitch Capabilities

Three-thread overlocking is the stretchy but resilient stitch that is basic to the majority of machines. Some serger customers want or need a more varied stitch repertoire. For instance: a 4-thread safety stitch overlock for durable stretchy seams, a 2-thread overedge for one-step flatlocking and delicate, narrow hemming, or a 5-thread chainstitch/overlock combination for the widest, most ravel-proof stable seams. (Serger stitches are illustrated and explained in the "Glossary of Stitches," pages 157-161).

What stitches you need depends on the fabrics and projects you sew. Because you work in tandem with your conventional sewing machine, continue to count on it for lockstitching seams that will be pressed open, applying lapped zippers, and topstitching. For further discussion, refer to "Considering a Five-Thread Serger?" on page 150.

Lighting

Lighting is built-in on most recent models. Ask not only if the model has a light, but where it is, how it's turned on, and if the illumination can be directed. Keep in mind that auxiliary lights (screw-on or free-standing) can be added to those sergers without lights or to augment built-in lighting.

Sewing Speed

Sewing speed may be an important factor for those involved in production sewing for a cottage industry, a dressmaking business, or a large family. (Also for "pedal to the metal" types who favor full-throttle stitching of any project.) Judge by test-serging. If accuracy at slower rates is crucial, look for dual speed and electronic controls.

Tension Adjustment

Inset tension dials and levers are a design trend, attributed to a streamlining of serger silhouettes. Knob or "beehive" dials are the other tension option. (Several companies are offering both inset and knob dial models. See Fig. 13-1 on page 146 for examples.) If tension adaptability is of paramount importance to you, test-serge using a wide variety of threads on scraps of your favorite fabrics. Do you have difficulty adjusting for a balanced tension, particularly if the fabric or thread is lightweight or heavy?

Disengageable Cutting

If the movable (usually upper) knife in the assembly can be moved out or away, it will stop the cutting action. (Serging cut-free might be helpful—for instance, when serging tucks or decorative flatlocking.) Actually, all cutters can be disengaged, but usually they can be disengaged more quickly if they can be done by hand than if they must be unscrewed. (With limited experience, serger-users can learn to guide the fabric cut-free, so disengageability becomes a less crucial factor.)

Stitch Length

Stitch length is variable on all overlock machines. Some stitch adjustments are made with a screwdriver, and some are dialed by hand. If you will frequently be converting back and forth between satin and longer serging, look for fast, easy length adjustability.

Stitch Width

Stitch width is variable to some degree on all machines by moving the cutter in or out (called narrowing or widening the "bite"). If this requires a screwdriver, many seamstresses shy away from the task. For speedier width changing, tool-free adjustments, such as dialing changes or changing needle positions or plates, are better alternatives.

If your serger will be a single-function appliance, i.e., used for serging seams in knits only, width variability won't be a priority. However, decorative serging demands stitch width flexibility and frequent adjustments; test the width-changing mechanism and range before buying.

Narrow Rolled Hems

Narrow rolled hems are made quickly and beautifully on a serger. Most sergers (but not all) can make a narrow rolled hem. Compare the rolled-hem conversion speed, stitch width, and quality from one prospective machine to another. Serger owners claim that this stitch alone "pays for their serger" in fast, professionally finished napkins, scarves, ruffles, and hems.

Differential Feed

Differential feed is the up-and-coming feature being touted by most serger companies. You will pay extra for this feature, so ask yourself: *"Will I use differential feeding enough to warrant the additional cost?"*

How it works: Two sets of feed dogs feed the fabric layer(s) in and out from under the extra-long serger foot. To prevent stretching of knits or loosely woven fabrics, you dial the highest (usually "2") setting, which means a 2:1 ratio. See Fig. 13-2. The

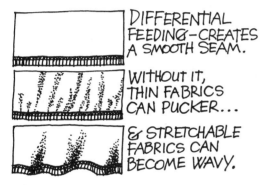

DIFFERENTIAL FEEDING—CREATES A SMOOTH SEAM.

WITHOUT IT, THIN FABRICS CAN PUCKER...

& STRETCHABLE FABRICS CAN BECOME WAVY.

Fig. 13-2

front set of feed dogs will feed in twice as much fabric as is released out from under the back of the foot. On lighter weights, use this setting for easing and gathering.

For taut sewing, to prevent puckering of lightweight or single-layer fabric (especially when satin-serging a narrow rolled edge), you dial the lowest (usually ".7") setting, which means a .7:1 ratio. See Fig. 13-2. The front set of feed dogs will feed in ".7" as much fabric as is released out from under the back of the foot. On stretch fabrics, use this setting for stretching while serging to flounce the edge.

Other Options

Optional feet and attachments may help surmount some of your sewing challenges. With few exceptions, blind-hem and elastic/tape applicator feet are available, sold as standard or optional accessories. Other intriguing feet, such as those for applying bead strands, piping, and binding, are now available for many models (see "Neat Feet," pages 139-141). Like sergers, it's best to test feet and attachments first, before buying.

Complementary Features

If you are adding to your collection (some of the nicest people own two or more sergers), look for different features. Many busy seamsters will invest in a second machine with the intention of using it exclusively for narrow rolled edging. So rather than shopping for the most features, look for the one or two you don't have or for the ones that on a new model would perform better than those on your current machine.

It Feels Good

"I don't know why but I just like it better" judgments should be as compelling as your assessment of a machine's features. After studying the market and test-serging, you'll probably like sewing with one serger better than another, even if, feature-by-feature, it's identical to the competition. Perhaps it's the color, the sounds, the design. Listen to your leanings— you'll find time to sew with a serger you love.

Considering a Five-Thread Serger?

Newest on the serger market are the 5-thread machines. The versatility of these multiple-stitch sergers is definitely intriguing. Remember, however, that the term *5-thread* describes the number of threads, not the number of stitches. Read all about the many interpretations of the term *5-thread*, then analyze if and how each variation of 5-thread would increase your sewing speed and quality. Follow the analysis guidelines below before you write your check for a new 5-thread serger.

• **Review the 5-thread models on the market.** As this book was going to press, the following 5-thread models are being sold, and each brand offers different stitch capabilities: the Bernette 335 from Bernina of America, the ElnaLock L-5, PRO-4, and PRO-5 from Elna, the Hobbylock 797 from Pfaff, and the Ultralock 14U85 and 14U65 from Singer. By the time you read this, there will be other 5-thread models offered in the fast-changing serger market. Inquire with dealers in your area.

The aforementioned models offer the conventionally designed 5-thread stitch: a combination of a 2-thread chainstitch and a 3-thread overlock, as shown on page 158. These stitches generally, but not always, can be used independently or together. (In fact, you might be attracted to a 5-thread machine because of its one-stitch-at-a-time variability, instead of the stitch combinations.)

• **Find out if the serger you now own can be adapted for 5-thread stitching.** A 5-thread adaptation for the classic White 534 Superlock has been promoted by White dealers. This conversion results in a 3/4-thread overlock with two threads threaded through the left needle (total: five threads). See Fig. 13-3.

Fig. 13-3

Some adaptations add extra stitch capability to a 5-thread repertoire. For instance, Elna offers a stitch conversion kit for the Elna L-5. The L-5 offers the versatility of five stitches: 5-thread seaming, 3-thread overlocking, true 4-thread seaming, 2-thread overedging, and 2-thread chainstitching. With the kit, the L-5 can also serge a 3/4-thread safety stitch. If you have an L-5, or are contemplating purchasing this Elna model, ask your dealer about this kit.

Five-thread adaptations for other models are on the horizon. Again, check with your dealer.

• **Survey the other multiple-stitch options.** Though it does not yet offer 5-threads, Tacony does offer Baby Lock sergers that combine 3/4-thread, 3-thread, and 2-thread stitch capabilities. Some sergers can be adapted for additional stitches; for example, the Huskylock (Viking) 535D, a 3/4-thread model, can be mechanically altered to add 2-thread overedging. Also, the White Superlock 216 can chainstitch or 3-thread overlock, but not simultaneously.

• **Decide which machine best suits your sewing needs.** Test-sew on prospective sergers. For testing, bring fabric scraps that represent a cross section of the projects you make.

Weigh the stretchability (double chain-stitch seams are the most stable), strength, width and length variability, and decorative applications for each stitch. Also, *how easily can you convert from one stitch to another? Will you actually use the extra stitches and features —enough to justify the price?* You will pay more for 5-thread and multiple-stitch serger models, but the sewing versatility gained may well be worth the extra cost.

Serger Cutting Attachments

Serger cutting action can be simulated by an attachment that replaces the foot on your conventional machine. Ask your dealer about such attachments. (Industry insiders say the demand for cutting attachments has paralleled serger popularity; evidently serger owners, spoiled by the timesaving overlock cutting action, also want to trim and stitch simultaneously on their conventional machine.) Bernina, Micro™-Serger USA, and Tacony all sell their own versions of the cutting attachment, and there's probably one to fit your conventional machine. Prices generally range from $40 to $80.

Designed for low, high, or slant shank zigzag machines, these attachments trim the raw edge of the fabric while sewing conventionally with the stitch of your choice (zigzag, overcast, or stretch stitches minimize tunneling).

The speed and stitch type (lockstitch) remain conventional, but these handy attachments do save trimming time while producing neater, more durable seams and finished edges. See Fig. 13-4.

"Mini-Serger" Attachment for Conventional Sewing Machines.

Fig. 13-4

Buying the Right Serger Needle

Quick—*what type of needle do you need for your serger?* Can't remember? If you must refer to your serger owner's manual, you're not alone. The numerous serger needles and their identifying systems (like DB x 1 and JL x 1) can be confusing. Also, several 4/2-thread (chainstitch/overedge combination) models require two different needle types for the right and left positions.

Conventional machine needles are usually interchangeable. *Serger needles, to date, are available in seven different needle systems*, ranging from industrial to conventional and including modified industrial and conventional needles. Serger sewing machines may be convenient and fast to use, but their needle systems haven't yet been simplified (all the more reason to be close to a good dealer).

When sergers were first introduced to the home sewing market, most models used **industrial needles**. These needles, available in four formats, are designed to withstand the stress of creating 1,300 or more stitches per minute. The top of the shank of a traditional industrial needle is round, not flat-sided, like regular sewing machine needles. The difference between the various industrial needles is in the position of the eye and the length. The length differences of these needles vary up to 1/4". Remember to insert the industrial needle with the scarf (the hollowed area above the needle eye) to the back (Fig. 13-5).

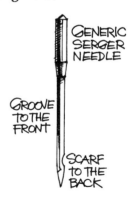

GENERIC SERGER NEEDLE

GROOVE TO THE FRONT

SCARF TO THE BACK

Fig. 13-5

As sergers evolved, many companies converted to using **conventional household sewing needles,** size 15 x 1. Sergers which use a 15 x 1 system make needle replacement convenient, as both conventional and serger machines use the same type. For their models that require household needles, many (not all) companies suggest Schmetz (130/750H—15 x 1) universal point H-series needles or the comparable Organ HA x 130 needles.

Now a third needle variation has been added. Several serger manufacturers are **customizing either the industrial or conventional needles** for their particular models. These specialty needles are listed in the "Serger Needle Guide" chart, pages 154-156.

Regardless of the needle type, the suggested needle sizes are generally limited to sizes 11 and 14 (or 70/75 and 90 in European sizing). Notions expert Nancy Zieman (of *Sewing with Nancy* television fame) explains, "We haven't noticed that the size of serger needles affects the stitch quality much. The tension and length settings are more important." (Serger repairperson Bruce Finfrock recommends size 12 or 14 [to accommodate all-purpose threads], rather than the standard size 11 needles that come in machines shipped from Japan. See his comments on page 144.)

☞ **Update tip:** When serging with heavier thread in the needle(s), the strand should be able to lie in the front needle groove for smoothest passage through the fabric. If the needle is too small in proportion to the thread, stitch formation may be difficult or irregular. Move up to a larger needle size, but no larger than that recommended by your owner's manual.

Unlike a needle in a conventional machine, if a serger needle is bent, nicked, or just plain worn out, it will not form a stitch. If stitches aren't forming correctly or at all, simply replacing the needle may solve the problem. Or, if holes are forming along the needleline, change to a new, perhaps smaller or ball-point needle. Keep an adequate supply of needles on hand, and double-check your owner's manual for the correct needle type and suggested sizes.

Needle update: Ball-point industrial serger needles, recommended by many experts for skip-free serging on knits, are now available. Ask your local dealer if they are in stock or can be ordered. The Nancy's Notions catalog includes ball-point industrial needles, in types DC x 1, BL x 1, and DC x 1F, all sized 11/70 and 14/90 (see "Serge-by-Mail Directory," page 166).

Also, attention White Superlock and Viking Huskylock 300-series owners: if you're having problems with skipped stitches, use Organ-brand "SP" needles. The Organ needles designated "SP" (after the size) are specially curved below the scarf to effectively eliminate this problem. Ask for them at your local dealer or through mail-order suppliers like Nancy's Notions, Serge & Sew Notions, and Sewing Emporium.

Serger Needle Guide

Keep this guide as a handy reference. There's room to add needle types for new models, as they are introduced.

Key

(r.n.): right needle

(l.n.): left needle

DC x 1F: a DC x 1 needle with a flat-back shank

Serger brand and model		Industrial			Conven-tional	Special
	DCx1	BLx1	DBx1	JLx1	15x1	(Customized)
Baby Lock (Tacony)	418 417 408 3200	605 625				DCx1F 5280ED 5180 738D 728 714 436
Bernette (Bernina)		204 (r.n.) 203		204 (l.n.)	335 334D 334 234	
Easy Lock (Simplicity)	800 600	550	803		843 804	DCx1F 880D 850
ElnaLock (Elna)					All models	ELX-705

(continued)

Serger brand and model		Industrial			Conven-tional	Special
	DCx1	BLx1	DBx1	JLx1	15x1	(Customized)
Elnita (Elna)					T-34 T-33	
FunLock (Bernina)					004 003	
Hobbylock (Pfaff)	603		796 795 (r.n.) 794 604	795 (l.n.)	786 784 783	
Homelock or Brother Lock (Brother)			M526-LCW (DBx1 for others not on this chart)		M760DE M760 760D M730D	
Huskylock (Viking)		440 430 435 535 535D			560ED 340D 340 300	
Juki Lock (Juki)		MO-134 MO-104N (r.n.) MO-103N		104N (l.n.)	MO-634D MO-634 MO-613	(continued)

Serger brand and model		Industrial			Conven-tional	Special
	DCx1	BLx1	DBx1	JLx1	15x1	(Customized)
MyLock (New Home)		779 778 777			Combi-DX 234D 234 203	
Riccar Lock (Riccar)	333	613 343DR 343			624	
SergeMate (Tacony)		5030 300			5040 432	
Superlock (White)					All models	
Ultralock (Singer)					Singer-2045 (Conven-tional) 14U64 14U53 14U52	Singer #2054 14U85 14U65 14U34 14U32 Singer #2053 14U13 14U12
Toyota (Fabri-Centers)					All models	

Glossary of Stitches

Stitch Configuration   Uses

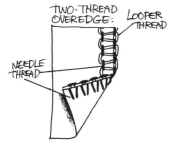

Fig. G-1

- Edge and seam finishing because the threads do not lock at the seamline.
- Flatlocking with minimal tension adjustments.
- Decorative or lightweight edge finishing.
- May have narrow rolled hemming capability.
- Usually part of a 4-, 2/3/4-, or 5-thread stitch.

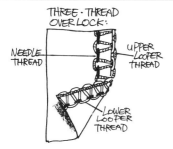

Fig. G-2

- Seaming—the threads lock at the seamline.
- Seaming and finishing stretchy fabrics.
- Flatlocking with tension adjustments.
- Finishing seams and edges.
- May have narrow rolled hem capability.
- Usually the one stitch offered on a basic machine or part of a 3/4-, 2/3/4-, or 5-thread stitch.

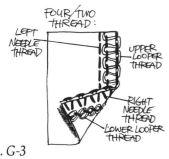

Fig. G-3

- Seaming with a wider allowance.
- Stable seams in ravely, loosely woven, and stretchy fabrics.
- Menswear, bridal fashions, jackets, and decorating projects that may need wider seam allowances or that may call for topstitching of the seam.
- Seam and edge finishing with the 2-thread overedge (drop the left needle).
- Decorative topstitching with the 2-thread chainstitching (drop the right needle).
- Overedge may have narrow rolled edge capability.
- May be the one stitch combination featured or a stitch option on a 5-thread machine.

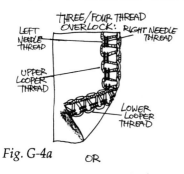

Fig. G-4a   OR

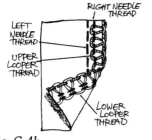

Fig. G-4b

- Similar to the 3-thread stitch, with an extra stitch running down the middle for added durability.
- Durable seaming and decorative finishing.
- Decorative flatlocking with tension adjustments. See page 49.
- Either or both needles can be used for seaming or finishing. Drop the left needle for a narrower 3-thread stitch, the right needle for a wider 3-thread stitch.
- May have narrow rolled hem capability (see page 48) using both or one (right) needle.
- The upper looper may interlock with the left needle (Fig. G-4a), called a safety stitch or may interlock with the right needle sometimes called a mock safety stitch, (Fig. G-4b).
- Usually the one stitch combination on a machine or a stitch option on a 2/3/4- or 5-thread machine.

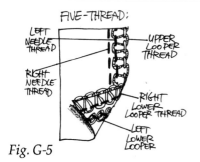

Fig. G-5

- All stitch uses described previously apply to those stitches that are part of the 5-thread: the 3-thread overlock and the 2-thread chainstitch.
- The most stable seaming and finishing.
- Generally stitch elements can be combined or used independently. Adjustments must be made to switch from one stitch to another.
- Often combined with other stitch options on a machine. See page 150.

Definitions of Other Stitch Terms

Changing thread tensions changes the look and functions of any stitch. The following stitches, created by tension adjustments, are mentioned throughout this book:

Balanced: On a 3- or 3/4-thread overlock stitch, when the upper and lower looper threads interlock at the edge of the fabric. On a 2-thread overedge stitch, when the needle and looper threads interlock at the edge of the fabric. (Figs. G-1 through G-5, above, are balanced-tension stitches.) See Fig. G-6.

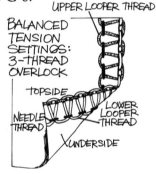

Fig. G-6

Flatlocked: On a 3- or 3/4-thread overlock stitch, when the needle thread is loosened enough to allow the serged fabric layers to be pulled flat. On a 2-thread overedge stitch very little tension adjustment, if any, is required to allow the serged fabric layers to be pulled flat; slight loosening of the needle thread may be helpful. Flat-locking will be flatter, if the stitches hang over the edge, halfway beyond the cut edge or fold, as shown. Refer to "Improved: Flatter Flatlocking," pages 49-50. Use either side of the stitch—the looper thread side (flatlock wrong sides together) or the needle thread

"ladder" side (flatlock right sides together). Seams, hems, or folds can be flatlocked. See Fig. G-7.

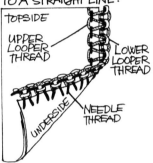

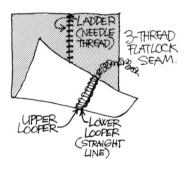

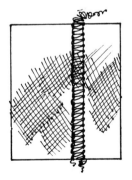

Fig. G-7

Faux flatlocking: Balanced-tension serging strategically positioned and edge-stitched to look like flatlocking. See pages 15-16.

Narrow rolled hem or edge: Requires the same tension adjustments as the reversible edge binding, above, except that the stitch width is narrowed and rolled by using a narrower stitch finger. See pages 113-114. On some sergers, adjustments for narrowing the stitch are built-in, while on others, special feet and/or plates are required. The amount of roll depends on the bite (the distance between the needle and the knife) in relation to the finger width; the wider the bite, the more the fabric will roll over the finger (see pages 136-139). Also, some fabrics roll more easily than others; light to mid-weight, crisp cotton wovens roll readily, whereas bottom-weight polyester gabardines resist rolling.

Note: A narrow hem can also be balanced. The stitch width is narrowed, but the tensions are balanced (see "Balanced," above.) See Fig. G-8.

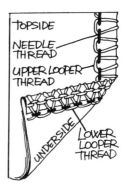

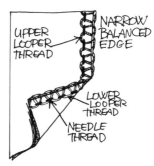

Fig. G-8

Reversible edge binding: On a 3-thread overlock stitch, when the lower looper thread is tightened enough to pull the upper looper thread completely over to the underside, encasing the edge; some loosening of the upper looper thread may be helpful. The lower looper will form a straight line on the underside of the stitch, along the needleline. On a 2-thread overedge stitch, when the needle thread is tightened enough to pull the looper thread completely over to the underside, encasing the edge; some loosening of the looper thread may be helpful. The looper thread will wrap to the needleline on the underside of the stitch. This stitch is popular for finishing jacket lapels and other projects that call for a stitch that looks the same on both sides. See Fig. G-9.

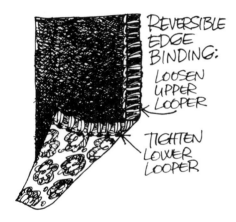

Fig. G-9

☞ **Update tip:** Use **ease-plus** to prevent stretching as you serge (or sew conventionally). With one index finger, hold the fabric behind the presser foot. With the other hand, force-feed the fabric under the foot, faster than the feed dogs are taking it in. (If your serger has differential feeding, ease-plussing is automatic; adjust for any setting above 1, up to 2.)

Use **taut serging** to prevent puckering as you serge (or sew conventionally). Hold the fabric edge taut in front of and behind the presser foot. (If your serger has differential feeding, taut serging is automatic; adjust for any setting below 1, usually .7.)

For more about differential feeding, see page 149.

Sources

Serger Companies
(brand names in parentheses)

Bernina of America (Bernette and FunLock)
534 West Chestnut
Hinsdale, IL 60521

Brother International Corporation (Homelock)
8 Corporate Place
Piscataway, NJ 08854

Elna, Inc. (ElnaLock and Elnita)
7642 Washington Ave. South
Eden Prairie, MN 55344

Fabri-Centers of America (Toyota)
23550 Commerce Road
Cleveland, OH 44122

Juki Industries of America (Juki Lock)
421 North Midland Ave.
Saddle Brook, NJ 07662

(West Coast office)
3555 Lomita Blvd., Suite H
Torrance, CA 90505

New Home Sewing Machine Company (MyLock and Combi)
100 Hollister Road
Teterboro, NJ 07608

Pfaff American Sales Corporation (Hobbylock)
610 Winters Ave.
Paramus, NJ 07653

Riccar America (Riccar Lock)
14281 Franklin Ave.
Tustin, CA 92680

Simplicity Sewing Machines (Easy Lock)
P.O. Box 56
Carlstadt, NJ 07072

Singer Sewing Machine Company (Ultralock)
North American Sewing
Products Division
135 Raritan Center Parkway
Edison, NJ 08837

Tacony Corporation (Baby Lock and SergeMate)
Babylock U.S.A.
P.O. Box 730
St. Louis, MO 63026

Viking Sewing Machine Company (Huskylock)
2300 Louisiana Ave. North
Minneapolis, MN 55427

White Sewing Machine Company (Superlock)
11750 Berea Road
Cleveland, OH 44111

Serge-by-Mail Directory

We recommend that every serger enthusiast develop a special relationship with his or her local dealers and retailers for convenient advice and inspiration, plus the ease of coordinating purchases. However, when specialty items cannot be found locally or when a homesewer lives several miles from a sewing retailer, mail-order specialists are a worthwhile option.

The following list will make your search for these resources a breeze. Each company is listed under just one category—its major product concentration related to serging—although the company may offer other merchandise or services. Our list is for reference only and does not carry our endorsement or guarantee. (We have not knowingly included any questionable items or firms.) Enjoy.

Risk-free Mail Order

• **Before you buy:** Read catalog descriptions carefully to make sure the product is what you want. Is there a guarantee? What is the policy for returns?

• **Placing your order:** Fill out the order form carefully and make a copy of both order and payment for future reference. Never send cash. When ordering by phone, complete the order form first to prevent mistakes. If possible, keep a record of the date of your phone order, as well as the name of the salesperson.

• **If there is a problem with your order:** Contact the company right away, by phone or by mail. If you contact by phone, be sure to record the time and date of your call, as well as the name of the contact person. Follow up in writing, describing the problem and outlining any solution reached during the phone call. Send copies of your order and payment record. Get a return receipt from the shipper when returning merchandise.

• **The "30-Day Rule":** If a delivery date isn't given in a company's materials, it must ship within 30 days of receiving your order (COD orders excepted), according to the Federal Trade Commission's Mail Order Merchandise Rule. If you place an order using a credit card, your account shouldn't be billed until shipment is made. If you send payment with your order and your order doesn't arrive when promised, you may cancel the order and get a full refund.

Authors' note: In today's volatile business climate, any mail-order source list will change frequently. Please send your comments on any out-of-business notifications or unsatisfactory service to *Update Newsletters*, 2269 Chestnut, Suite 269-BK, San Francisco, CA 94123.

Key to Abbreviations and Symbols:

SASE = Self-addressed, stamped (first class) envelope

L-SASE = Large SASE (2-oz. first class postage)

* = refundable with order

= for information, brochure or catalog

✎ **Note:** Check with your postmaster regarding Canadian mail.

Specialty Patterns and Designs

✎ **Note:** Patterns from the major companies (Butterick, McCall's, New Look, Simplicity, and Vogue) are readily available from your local fabric stores.

Ghee's, 106 E. Kings Highway, Suite 205, Shreveport, LA 71104, 318/868-1154. Patterns and notions for making handbags. $1#.

Great Fit Patterns, 221 S.E. 197th, Portland, OR 97233, 503/665-3125. Fashionable styles created exclusively for the large figure, sizes 38-60. $1#.

Jean Hardy Patterns, 2151 La Cuesta Dr., Santa Ana, CA 92705. Patterns for riding, cheerleading, skating and square dancing. $1#.

Kwik-Sew Pattern Co., Inc., 3000 Washington Ave., N., Minneapolis, MN 55411, 612/521-7651.

Kwik-Sew Patterns (Canada), Ltd., 5035 Timberlea Blvd., Unit #7, Mississauga, Ontario L4W 2W9 Canada, 416/625-0135. Easy-to-sew fashions for the whole family. Choose from 800 patterns. $3.50# ($4 in Canada).

Logan Kits, Route 3, Box 380, Double Springs, AL 35553, 205/486-7732. Lingerie and activewear kits for men, women, and children. $1 and L-SASE#.

Peg's Fabric and Yarn Closet, 4110 Callfield Road, Wichita Falls, TX 76308. Peg's Pieces patterns. SASE#.

Picks Fine Handwovens, 3316 Circle Hill Rd., Alexandria, VA 22305. Handwoven silk skirt lengths and matching sweater yarns packaged with lining, notions and sewing/knitting instructions. Swatches, $2.

Pineapple Appeal, P.O. Box 197, Owatonna, MN 55060, 507/455-3041. Sweatshirts, jams, pillows, windsocks and tote bags kits for the beginner sewer. Free#.

Prime Moves, P.O. Box 8022, Portland, OR 97207. Authentic aerobic wear. $1#.

Raindrop & Roses, 8 SE 199 Ave., Portland, OR 97233. Maternity and nursing wear patterns. $1#.

Seams Sew Easy, P.O. Box 2189, Manasses, VA 22110. Swimwear patterns (two-piece). L-SASE#.

Serging Ahead, P.O. Box 45, Grandview, MO 64030. Serger patterns and supplies. $1#.

Stretch & Sew Inc., P.O. Box 185, Eugene, OR 97440. Multisized patterns for women, men and children. Free#.

Sunrise Designs, Box 277, Dept. SU, Orem, UT 84059. Infant, toddler and children's patterns. Several easy-to-sew designs in each multi-sized pattern. Free#.

Susan's Sewing Center, 68-720 Highway 11, Cathedral City, CA 92234. Patterns by the Yard. L-SASE#.

U-Sew-Knits, P.O. Box 43078, Phoenix, AZ 85080. Pre-cut women's sportswear and children's clothing kits. SASE#.

Yes Mam Lingerie & Fashions, 106 S. Third Street, Leesburg, FL 32748. Kits for lingerie, men's lounge wear and women's fashions. $1 and SASE#.

Lace, Trims, Ribbons, Bead Strands, Sequins and Glitz

Badhir Trading, Inc., 8429 Sisson Hwy.-S2, Eden, NY 14057, 716/992-3193. Appliqués, bead/pearl fringe, sequins, and jewels for bridal and evening wear. $2*#.

Baubanbea Enterprises, Box 1205, Smithtown, NY 11787. Rhinestones, sequins, beads, jewels, lace, appliqués, feathers, silk flowers, fabrics, and more. $4#.

Collections, P.O. Box 806, Ithaca, NY 14851. Laces, 3/8" to 60" wide, including Rose Garden, Point d'esprit, lingerie, stretch and fiberfill lace. Free#.

Creative Trims, 18 Woodland Drive, Lincroft, NJ 07738. Lace, embroideries and ribbons. Free#.

Donna Lee's Sewing Center, 25234 Pacific Hwy. S., Kent, WA 98032, 206/941-9466. Imported laces and Swiss embroideries; silk ribbons and French trims; Swiss batiste and China silks. $3#.

Elsie's Exquisiques, 513 Broadway, Niles, MI 49120, 616/684-7034. French-reproduction laces, trims, silk ribbons, hand-crafted ribbon roses, and insertion laces.

Greatest Sew on Earth, P.O. Box 214, Fort Tilden, NY 11695. Sequin and jeweled trims and appliqués, eyelet embroideries, bridal laces, and pearls. $1#.

Lace Place, 9250 N. 43rd Ave., Ste. 6, Glendale, AZ 85302. Assorted laces. $2#.

Lace Plus, Inc., P.O. Box 3243-U, Fort Lee, NJ 07024. Fine quality Schiffli laces in a variety of widths and designs. $2# w/swatches.

Pioneer Specialty Products, Box 412, Holden, MA 01520. Laces, ribbons, eyelet, tape. $1*#.

Great Serger Notions

Aardvark Adventures, P.O. Box 2449, Livermore, CA 94551, 415/443-2687. Books, beads, buttons, bangles, plus unusual assortment of related products. Decorative serging thread, including metallics. $1#.

The Bee Lee Company, P.O. Box 36108-B, Dallas, TX 75235. Complete selection of threads, zippers, notions and trims, including Western styles. Free#.

Bobette Industries, 2401 S. Hill St., Los Angeles, CA 90007-2785, toll-free in CA, 800/237-6462 (orders only). Notions, tools, threads, books, machine parts, and accessories. $1#.

Catherine's, Rt. 6, Box 1227, Lexington, NC 27292, 704/798-1595. Serger threads and more at wholesale prices. Minimum order, $35. School quantity discounts. $2 and L-SASE for thread color card.

Clotilde, Inc., 1909 SW First Ave., Ft. Lauderdale, FL 33315, 305/761-8655. Catalog of over 1,200 items, including special serger threads and notions, sewing tools and supplies, books and videos. $1#.

Custom Zips, P.O. Box 1200, So. Norwalk, CT 06856. Zippers cut to order. $2#.

The Cutting Edge, P.O. Box 76044, St. Peters, MO 63376. Serger notions, including coned threads (all-purpose and decorative), needle threaders, patterns and carrying cases. L-SASE#.

D & E Distributing, 199 N. El Camino Real #F-242, Encinitas, CA 92024. Decorative threads and yarns, including silk, rayon, and Madeira metallics. L-SASE#.

The Embroidery Stop, 1042 Victory Dr., Yardley, PA 19067. Threads, yarns, needles. $1#.

Fit For You, 781 Golden Prados Dr., Diamond Bar, CA 91795, 714/861-5021. Sewing notions, serger accessories, videos, and square dance patterns. L-SASE#.

Home-Sew, Dept. S, Bethlehem, PA 18018. Basic notions, trims, coned serger threads, and tools. Free#.

Jacquart's, 505 E. McLeod, Ironwood, MI 49938, 906/932-1339. Zippers. $1#.

Maryland Trims, P.O. Box 3508, Silver Springs, MD 20901. Laces, sewing notions and supplies. $1.75#.

Mill End Store, Box 02098, Portland, OR 97202, 503/236-1234. Broad selection of notions, trims, serger threads, and accessories. SASE#.

Nancy's Notions, Ltd., P.O. Box 683, Beaver Dam, WI 53916, 414/887-0391. Over 300 sewing notions and accessories, serger threads and tools, interfacings and fabrics, books and videos. Free#.

National Thread & Supply, 695 Red Oak Rd., Stockbridge, GA 30281, 800/ 847-1001, ext. 1688; in GA, 404/389-9115. Name brand sewing supplies and notions. Free#.

Newark Dressmaker Supply, P.O. Box 2448, Lehigh Valley, PA 18001, 215/ 837-7500. Sewing notions, trims, buttons, decorative threads, and serger supplies. Free#.

The Perfect Notion, 566 Hoyt St., Darien, CT 06820, 203/968-1257. Hard-to-find notions and serger threads (including their exclusive Thread-Fuse™ melt adhesive thread). $1#.

Serge and Sew Notions, 11761 99th Ave. N., Maple Grove, MN 55369, 612/ 493-2449. Serger threads, books, patterns, furniture, fabrics, and more, priced 20-40% below retail. Free#. Swatch club, $6 for six months.

Serging Ahead, P.O. Box 45, Grandview, MO 64030. Serger threads, books, and patterns. $1#.

Sew-Art International, P.O. Box 550, Bountiful, UT 84010. Decorative threads, notions, and accessories. Free#.

Sew Craft, P.O. Box 1869, Warsaw, IN 46580, 219/269-4046. Books, decorative threads, and notions.

Sew-Fit Co., P.O. Box 565, LaGrange, IL 60525, 312/579-3222. Sewing notions and accessories; modular tables for serger/sewing machine setup; books. Free#.

Sewing Emporium, 1087 Third Ave., Chula Vista, CA 92010, 619/420-3490. Hard-to-find sewing notions, sewing machine and serger cabinets and accessories, serger threads and accessories. $2#.

The Sewing Place, 100 West Rincon Ave., Suite 105, Dept. UX189, Campbell, CA 95008. Sewing machine and serger needles and feet, plus books by Gale Grigg Hazen. Specify your brand and model if ordering machine accessories. L-SASE#.

The Sewing Workshop, 2010 Balboa St., San Francisco, CA 94121, 415/221-SEWS. Unique designer notions. L-SASE#.

Solo Slide Fasteners, Inc., P.O. Box 528, Stoughton, MA 02072, 800/343-9670. All types and lengths of zippers, other selected notions. Free#.

Speed Stitch, 3113-D Broadpoint Dr., Harbor Heights, FL 33983. Machine art kits and supplies, including all-purpose, decorative, and specialty serging threads, books, and accessories. $3*#.

Threads & Things, P.O. Box 83190, San Diego, CA 92138, 619/440-8760. 100% rayon thread. Free#.

Thread Discount & Sales, 7105 S. Eastern, Bell Gardens, CA 90201, 213/562-3438. Coned polyester thread. SASE#.

Threads West, 422 E. State St., Redlands, CA 92373, 714/793-4405 or 0214. Coned thread, serger parts, and accessories. SASE for free thread color list.

Treadleart, 25834 Narbonne Ave., Ste. I, Lomita, CA 90717, 800/327-4222. Books, serging supplies, notions, decorative threads, and creative inspiration. $1.50#.

T- Rific Products Co., P.O. Box 911, Winchester, OR 97495. Coned serger thread. Thread color chart, $1.25.

Two Brothers, 1602 Locust St., St. Louis, MO 63103. Zipper assortment. SASE#.

YLI Corporation, 45 West 300 North, Provo, UT 84601, 800/854-1932 or 801/377-3900. Decorative, specialty, serger, and all-purpose threads, yarns and ribbons. $1.50#.

Sensational Silks

Fabric Fancies, P.O. Box 50807, Reno, NV 89513. White silks, satins and jacquards for wedding gowns and lingerie. Imported laces, English illusion, and French net. $10# w/swatches.

Oriental Silk Co., 8377 Beverly Blvd., Los Angeles, CA 90048, 213/651-2323. Tussahs, chiffons, voiles, brocades, velvets, and more. Samples, $1*/for each fabric type specified.

Sureway Trading, 826 Pine Ave. #5, Niagara Falls, NY 14301, 716/282-4887. Silk fabrics and threads; silk/wool blends. Samples: naturals/whites, $8; colors, $12.

Thai Silks, 252 State St., Los Altos, CA 94022, 800/722- SILK; in CA, 800/221- SILK. Every type of silk imaginable. Fabric club, $10/year (three swatched mailings). Full swatch set (over 600), $20 ($18*).

Top Drawer Silks Ltd., 1938 Wildwood, Glendale Heights, IL 60139. Range of silk fabrications. Annual membership, $13# w/swatches.

Utex Trading, 710 Ninth St., Ste. 5, Niagara Falls, NY 14301, 416/596-7565. Silk fabrics, yarns and threads. Complete sample set, $35*.

Materials for Formals, Proms and Weddings

Bridal-by-the-Yard, P.O. Box 2492, Springfield, OH 45501. Imported and domestic laces and fabrics. $7# w/ swatches.

Bridal Elegance, 1176 Northport Dr., Columbus, OH 43235. Bridal Elegance patterns, sizes 4-22, and Wedding Gown Design Book. $.50#.

Bridals International, 45 Albany St., Cazenovia, NY 13035. Imported laces and fabrics; button loops and covered buttons for wedding gowns. $7.50*#.

La Sposa Veils, 252 West 40th Street, New York, NY 10018 212/354-4729 or 944-9142. Bridal headpieces. $3*#.

Mylace, P.O. Box 13466, Tallahassee, FL 32317, 800/433-8859; in FL, 800/433-8857. Extensive selection of trim and French bridal laces from 1/4" to 50" wide. $3.50#.

Patty's Pincushion, Inc., at Grande Affaires, 710 Smithfield St., Pittsburgh, PA 15219, 412/765-3010. Fabrics for the bridal party plus personalized service for planning wedding gowns. Swatches available.

Sew Elegant, 15461 Dorian St., Sylmar, CA 91342. Custom wedding gown kits, containing fabrics, laces, notions and multi-sized pattern. $5*# w/swatches.

S-T-R-E-T-C-H and Knit Fabrics

ABC Knits, 13315 433rd Court, S.E., North Bend, WA 98045 Acrylic, cotton, and wool blend knits; coordinated ribbing. L-SASE#.

Artknits by Clifford, 2174 Gary Rd., Traverse City, MI 49684, 616/943-8218. Custom-knit ribbing. SASE#.

Bead Different, 1627 S. Tejon, Colorado Springs, CO 80906, 303/473-2188. Stretch fabrics for dancers, skaters, and gymnasts. Send SASE with inquiry.

Beth McLeod, 1113 87th St., Daly City, CA 94015, 415/992-8731. Cotton/Lycra® and nylon/Lycra® stretch knits. $1 and SASE#.

Cottons Etc., 228 Genesee St., Oneida, NY 13421, 315/363-6834. Knits, sweatshirting, Lycra®, and more. L-SASE# w/swatches.

Golden Needles, 2320 Sauber Ave., Rockford, IL 61103. Custom-knit sweater yardage, sweater bodies with knitted name, and ribbing. Free swatches.

Kieffers Lingerie Fabrics & Supplies, 1625 Hennepin Ave., Minneapolis, MN 55403. Swimwear nylon/cotton Lycra®- blend stretch knits, sweatshirting, lingerie tricot. Also, many coned serger threads at bargain prices. Free#.

LG Fashions and Fabrics, P.O. Box 58394, Renton, WA 98058. Lycra®- blend knits of cotton and nylon. $2*# w/swatches.

Marianne's Textile Products (formerly Diversified Products), Box 319, RD 2, Rockwood, PA 15557. Sweater bodies, ribbing, knit collars. $2 and L-SASE#.

Rosen & Chadick, 246 West 40th St., New York, NY 10018. Cotton/Lycra® and nylon/Lycra® stretch knits. SASE#.

Sew Natural —Fabrics by Mail, Route 1, Box 428-C, Middlesex, NC 27557. Offers a wide range of knit fabrics (over thirty colors of cotton interlock), notions, and patterns. L-SASE# (w/swatches, add $2).

Sew Smart, P.O. Box 776, Longview, WA 98632. Ribbed knit collars, trims, and snaps. L-SASE#.

Stretch & Sew Fabrics, 1165 Valley River Drive, Eugene, OR 97401. Stretch & Sew patterns, plus a complete assortment of knit fabrics and notions. Also, serger thread. L-SASE#.

Stretch & Sew Fabrics, 19725 40th Ave. West, Lynnwood, WA 98036. A complete selection of knits, Stretch & Sew patterns and related notions. L-SASE#.

The Thrifty Needle, 3232 Collins St., Philadelphia, PA 19134. Sweater bodies and ribbing. $2 and SASE# w/ swatches.

Cycling, Hiking, Dancing, and Skiing Materials

Altra, Inc., 100 E. Washington St., New Richmond, IN 47967, 317/339-4653. Precut and pattern sportswear kits for outdoor activities, including skiing, backpacking, and cycling; skiwear fabrics and fleece; outerwear hardware and supplies. $1#.

DK Sports, Daisy Kingdom, 134 N.W. 8th, Portland, OR 97209, 503/222-9033. Kits and patterns for active sportswear and outerwear (skiing, bicycling, aerobics, swimwear and rainwear). Outerwear fabrics, including Taslan, mountain cloth, Cordura, Gore-tex, and vertical stretch ski pant fabric. $2#.

Donner Designs, Box 7217, Reno, NV 89510. Outerwear and activewear kits featuring water-repellent fabrics. Outerwear fabrics, including Tasnylon, one- and two-way stretch, and Gore-tex. Teacher discounts. $1#.

Frostline Kits, 2512 W. Independent Ave., Grand Junction, CO 81505, 800-KITS USA. Fabrics and precut kits for sportswear, outdoor clothing, luggage, camping gear, and more. Free#.

Green Pepper, Inc., 941 Olive, Eugene, OR 97407, 503/345-6665. Active and outerwear patterns and fabrics, including nylon/Lycra® and polypropylene/Lycra® knits, water-repellent fabrics, and insulating battings. $2#.

The Rain Shed, 707 N.W. 11th, Corvallis, OR 97330. Large selection of outerwear fabrics, kits, sewing notions, and tools. $1#.

Sundown Kits, 23815 43rd Ave. So., Kent, WA 98032-2856. Kits for assorted outerwear. $1#.

Timberline Sewing Kits, Inc., Box 126-SUB, Pittsfield, NH 03263, 603/435-8888. Fabrics and kits for outerwear and gear. $1#.

A Closetful of Fabrics

Baer Fabrics, 515 E. Market St., Louisville, KY 40202 800/288-2237; 502/583-5521. Comprehensive selection of fabrics. Seasonal sample sets (prices vary). Custom swatching available. Notions, $2#.

Britex-by-Mail, 146 Geary, San Francisco, CA 94108, 415/392-2910. Designer fabrics, including unusual sweater knits. Personalized swatching and special offerings. L-SASE#.

Camille Enterprises, P.O. Box 615-N, Rockaway, NJ 07866. Variety of fabrics, from the usual to designer. Four swatch mailings a year, $3 each; $10* a set.

Carolina Mills Factory Outlet, Box V, Hwy 76 West Branson, MO 65616, 417/334-2291. Designer fabrics from major sportswear manufacturers, 30-50% below regular retail. Sample swatches, $2.

Classic Cloth, 2508-D McMullen Booth Rd., Dept. UN, Clearwater, FL 34621, 813/799-0417. Austrian boiled wool, dyed-to-match wool trim, and coordinating paisley challis. Swatches, $5* a set.

Clearbrook Woolen Shop, P.O. Box 8, Clearbrook, VA 22624 703/662-3442. Variety of fabrics with emphasis on wool; 8-10 sample sets per year. Send name and address.

The Cloth Cupboard, P.O. Box 2263, Boise, ID 83701, 208/345-5567. Japanese wood-block prints. Swatches, $2.50 and SASE.

The Couture Touch, P.O. Box 681278, Dept. UN, Schaumburg, IL 60168, 312/310-8080. Famous-name fashion fabrics, including Anglo, Landau, and Logantex. Complimentary seasonal swatch collection available.

Creative Fabrics, 3303 Long Beach Rd., Oceanside, NY 11572. Fine wool and polyester suitings, silk and silky polyesters and challis. Swatches, $5*; $7 Canadian.

Creative Line Fabric Club, 101 Tremont St., Boston, MA 02108, 617/426-1473. Exclusive Italian imports, all natural fibers: silks, wools, cashmere, linens. Annual membership $25 (Canada, $35)—three swatch collections.

Cy Rudnick's Fabrics, 2450 Grand, Kansas City, MO 64108, 816/842-7808. Extensive collection of designer and specialty fabrics. Swatching service available. $3* and personal color and fabric request.

Designer's Touch, 7689 Lakeville Hwy., Petaluma, CA 94952, 707/778-8550. Imported and domestic designer fabrics offered through representatives nationwide. Fashion Club membership also available—$50/year for 9-10 mailings of swatched fashion portfolios.

Elegance Fabrics, 91A Scollard St., Toronto, Ontario M5R IG4 Canada, 416/966-3446. Finest European fabrics —wools, silks, linens, cottons. Seasonal swatch catalogs: 300-swatch edition, $60*; 460 swatches plus notions, $100*; 460 larger swatches plus notions, $150*.

Exquisite Fabrics, Inc. (formerly Watergate Fabrics), Dept. SUB, 1775 K Street NW, 1st Floor, Washington, DC 20006, 202/775-1818. Exclusive fabrics from France, Switzerland, and Italy: exquisite bridal fabrics and laces, silks, cashmeres, cottons, and worsted woolens. Complimentary swatching service.

The Fabric Club, P.O. Box 28126, Atlanta, GA 30358. Exclusive designer fabrics at a 50-75% savings. Annual membership, $8, for four coordinated fabric brochures.

Fabric Gallery, 146 W. Grand River, Williamston, MI 48895, 517/655-4573. Imported and domestic silks, wools, cottons, and better synthetics. $5/year for four swatched mailings.

Fabrications Fabric Club, Box 2162, South Vineland, NJ 08360. Fabrics from designers, ready-to-wear manufacturers, and mills. Four mailings, $10/year ($5*).

Fabrics in Vogue, 200 Park Ave., Suite 303 East, New York, NY 10166. Imported wools, silks, linens, cottons, and blends featured in Vogue Patterns. Six swatch mailings, $10/year.

Fabrics Unlimited, 5015 Columbia Pike, Arlington, VA 22204, 703/671-0324. Better fashion fabrics from designer cutting rooms.

Fabricland, Inc., Box 20235, Portland, OR 97220, 800/255-5412. Full bolts of fabric or boxes of notions available. Minimum order, $50. Write for price list.

Fashion Fabrics Club, 10490 Baur Blvd., St. Louis, MO 63132. Variety of quality designer and name-brand fabrics at moderate prices. Swatches monthly, $7/year.

Field's Fabrics, 1695 44th S.E., Grand Rapids, MI 49508, 616/455-4570. Ultrasuede®, Facile®, Caress®, and Ultraleather® swatches, $10; silk, Pendleton® wool, metallics and more (write for swatch information.)

Four Seasons Fabric Club, 811 E. 21st St., North Vancouver, BC V7J 1N8 Canada. Coordinated fabric selections identified by personal color season; $25/year for four swatch mailings.

G Street Fabrics, 11854 Rockville Pike, Rockville, MD 20852, 301/231-8998. Extensive selection of better fabrics. Over 20 basic fabric charts available, including cotton, wool, silk, Ultrasuede®, Facile® ($10 each). Sample subscription ($35/six months, $50/year) for 60 swatches per month. Custom sampling, $1/garment. Notions, $4#. Professional discounts.

Ginette's Haute Couture Fabrics, 36 Charles St., Milton, Ontario L9T 2G6 Canada. Cottons, linens, silks, denims, and easy-care blends at a savings of 20% to 50% off regular retail prices. Two catalogs, $15 Canadian/year.

Grasshopper Hill Fabrics, 224 Wellington St., Kingston, Ontario K7K 2Y8 Canada, 613/548-3889. Fine fabrics at competitive prices. Semiannual catalog, $5 Canadian ($2.50*).

House of Laird, 521 Southland Dr., P.O. Box 23778, Lexington, KY 40523, 606/276-5258. Designer fabrics offered through fabric showings by representatives nationwide. Write or call for information.

Imaginations, 32 Concord St., Framingham, MA 01701, 800/343-6953. Discounts on coordinated groupings of knits and wovens, many from top label cutting rooms. Yearly subscription, $10 (Canada, $15).

J. J. Products Ltd., 117 W. Ninth St., Suite 111, Los Angeles, CA 90015, 213/624-1840. Imported wool at discount prices. Swatch cards, $3* each.

Jehlor Fantasy Fabrics, 730 Andover Park West, Seattle, WA 98188, 206/575-8250. Variety of stretch fabrics, $2.50#. Baubles, Bangles and Beads catalog, $2.50. Ballroom dance costume patterns. SASE#.

Kasuri Dyeworks, 1959 Shattuck Ave., Berkeley, CA 94701, 415/841-4509. Fabrics from Japan. $5*#.

Left Bank Fabric Co. by Mail, 8354 W. Third St., Los Angeles, CA 90048, 213/655-7289. European silks, wools, cottons. Membership, $25*/year, for three collections.

Maxine Fabrics, 62 West 39th St. #902, New York, NY 10018, 212/391-2282. Moygashel linens and blends, Liberty prints, Ultrasuede® and Facile®, coordinated silks, cottons, and novelties. $3# w/swatches.

Natural Fiber Fabric Club, 521 Fifth Ave., New York, NY 10175. 100% wools, cottons, silks and linens at 20% savings over regular retail. Membership, $10/year for four swatched mailings and basic 24-fabric portfolio.

Oppenheim's, Dept. 394, N. Manchester, IN 46962, 219/982-6848. Classic, fashion fabrics at a savings. Swatches, $2*. Free swatch mailing after first order.

Portfolio Fabrics, 4984 Manor St., Vancouver, BC V5R 3Y2 Canada. Bi-monthly portfolios of imported fine fabric swatches. SASE#.

Samuel Lehrer & Co., 7 Depinedo Ave., Stamford, CT 06902. Fine clothing fabrics, primarily menswear. Swatch kit of over 50 samples, $9.95.

Seventh Avenue Designer Fabric Club, 701 Seventh Ave., Ste. 900, New York, NY 10036. Fabric selections from top-name Seventh Avenue designers at discount prices. Membership, $10/year for four swatched mailings.

Sew Easy Textiles & Trims, P.O. Box 54, Hudson Bay, SK S0E 0Y0 Canada, 306/865-3343. Quality fabrics, low prices. Volume discounts. Notions and patterns. $5# w/swatches.

References

Serger Books

The following are titles that were released after the publication of *Creative Serging Illustrated* (an extensive, complementary list is included in that book on page 154).

✎ **Note:** This book can be ordered for $16.95 ($18.00 for CA residents) postpaid from Open Chain Publishing (see address, below).

The Busy Woman's Sewing Book, by Nancy Zieman, ©1988, Open Chain Publishing (see address under *Creative Serging Illustrated,* below). Not a serger book, per se, but several serged methods are included. A wonderfully uncomplicated approach. $12 postpaid ($12.65 for CA residents).

Creative Serging Illustrated, by Pati Palmer, Gail Brown, and Sue Green, ©1987, Palmer/Pletsch Inc. A compilation of the creative basics that served as a starting point for the serger innovations presented in this book. Available from Open Chain Publishing, P.O. Box 2634-BK, Menlo Park, CA 94026 for $16.95 ($18 for CA residents) postpaid.

Distinctive Serger Gifts and Crafts, An Idea Book for All Occasions, by Naomi Baker and Tammy Young, ©1989, Chilton Book Company, Radnor, PA 19089. Clever, fast-to-serge projects that incorporate serged seaming, finishing and embellishing. $16.95 postpaid ($18 for CA residents) from Open Chain Publishing (see address, above).

French Sewing by Serger, by Kathy McMakin, ©1988, Albright & Co., Inc., P.O. Box 2011, Huntsville, AL 35804. Darling gifts and children's wear projects, all which utilize fast heirloom sewing (the serged adaptation of French handsewing). $11.50 postpaid.

Serger Idea Book, by Ann Hesse Price, ©1989, Palmer/Pletsch Inc., P.O. Box 12046, Portland, OR 97212-0046. Over 100 garments featured in lavish color photography illustrate a multitude of creative serging applications. Available at fabric stores and dealerships. Or available from the publisher for $16.20 postpaid.

Simplicity's Simply the Best Sewing Book, ©1988, Simplicity Pattern Co., 200 Madison Ave., New York, NY 10016. One of the best efforts to integrate serging and conventional sewing how-to's. The spiral-bound paperback is $16.45 postpaid from Simplicity, 901 Wayne St., Niles, MI 49121.

Singer Sewing Reference Library's Sewing with Sergers, coauthored by Karen Drellich and Sue Green, ©1989, Cy DeCosse, P.O. Box 3040, 5900 Green Oak Drive, Minnetonka, MN 55343. Full of captivating close-up color photography and solid information. Excellent troubleshooting reference. $14.95 postpaid.

Stylish Serging I, by Ervena Yu, ©1987, by Ervena's Place, 211 Bayside Place, Bellingham, WA 98225. The author's first book (in a larger 123-page format), covering pattern modifications and ingenious decorative serging. $16.50 postpaid.

Stylish Serging II, III and *IV,* by Ervena Yu, ©1989, by Ervena's Place (see address, above). More from this well-known authority on serged embellishments. Each of the three 32-page books features new garments created using Ervena's distinctive brand of serged appliqué, flatlocking, couching, tucking, and pleating. $9.50 postpaid per title (shipping is $2 total if you purchase all three titles).

Update Newsletter Serger Booklets

The following are *Update Newsletter* publications. They are sold by fabric stores, machine dealers, and mail-order sewing supply companies. Or you can order individual titles for $3.95 each from the *Update Newsletters,* 2269 Chestnut, #269, San Francisco, CA 94123.

Beyond Finishing: Innovative Serging, by Naomi Baker, ©1988. A concise, up-to-the minute report on decorative serging: serged lace, fish-line ruffles, tucked and rolled edges, and much more.

Know Your Serger, by Sue Green, ©1988. This best-selling booklet is a maintenance and troubleshooting guide for all serger brands and models. For beginners and experts alike.

Serged Bathroom, by Barb Griffin, ©1989. Learn how to transform any bathroom with fast-serged fabric decorating. Patternless projects include draped shower curtains, a flatlocked valance, and a monogrammed towel (ten projects total).

Serging for Special Occasions, by Ann Beyer, ©1988. A talented dressmaker's secrets for serging the fastest, most professional evening, prom, and wedding fashions.

Serged Gifts, in Minutes! by Tammy Young, ©1988. Charming projects that can be made in an hour or less—like a ruffled hanger, an upholstered basket, and a firewood carrier (nine projects total). No pattern purchases required.

Serging Lingerie, by Naomi Baker, ©1988. Learn to serge luxurious lingerie out of both knits and wovens. Edge-finishing and seaming are so easy, most are under-an-hour projects.

Serging Stretch Fashions, by Gail Brown, ©1989. Learn how to serge the *Lycra*®-blends (even if you're a rookie), from determining the stretch ratio to fast elastic finishings.

Serging Sweaters, by Naomi Baker ©1988. How to select the right fabrics, make your own pattern from a ready-made favorite, plus pro tips for cutting, seaming, and finishing.

Serger Videos

Your video library should include at least the tape specific to your serger brand. With few exceptions, most serger companies have produced one or more videos; some come with the machine, while others are sold separately. Inquire with your dealer.

Other training tapes deserving your consideration are being produced, sold, and rented by freelance serger specialists. Some are listed below. You'll find lots of timesaving information that's not brand-specific. (A particular brand will be used for technique demonstration rather than for promotional purposes.) If you're interested in any of these videos, ask for them at your local stores and dealers; for those unable to locate them at retail outlets, direct-order addresses and prices are given.

Contemporary Serging, ©1987, Nancy's Notions, Ltd., P.O. Box 683, Beaver Dam, WI 53916. Time: 60 minutes. Machines used: Hobbylock 794 and 795. $26.95 postpaid (transcript, $2.95). Rental, $6/week for Video Club members.

Creative Serging, ©1989, Palmer/Pletsch Inc., P.O. Box 12046, Portland, OR 97212-0046. Time: 60 minutes. Machines used: all brands. $31.20 postpaid. (Also look for the soon-to-be-released, *Creative Serging II.*)

Generic Serger Video I, ©1988, Live Guides, 10306 64th Place West, Everett, WA 98204. Time: 2 hours. Machines used: all the major brands sold—nine total. For sale ($62 postpaid) or rent ($14.50/ten days).

Knit, Serge & Sew, ©1987, Nancy's Notions, Ltd. (see address under *Contemporary Serging,* above). Time: 60 minutes. Machines used: Hobbylock 794 and 795. $26.95 postpaid (transcript, $2.95). Rental, $6/week for Video Club members.

Knits Are for Kids, ©1989 Sewing Update Videos, P.O. Box 31715, St. Louis, MO 63131. Time: 60 minutes. Machines used: Baby Lock 738D. $21.95 postpaid.

Luxurious Lingerie, ©1989, Sewing Update Videos (see address under *Knits Are for Kids,* above). Time: 60 minutes. Machines used: Baby Lock 738D. $21.95 postpaid.

Sensational Swimwear, ©1989, Sewing Update Videos (see address above). Time: 60 minutes. Machine used: Baby Lock 738D. $21.95 postpaid.

Sergers, The Basics and Serger Construction Methods, ©1986, University of Idaho, Moscow, ID, 83843. Time: 23 minutes each tape. Machine used: Baby Lock 418. To buy both titles, send $69.50 (or rent for $40/two weeks).

Serging and Sewing Activewear, ©1986, Nancy's Notions, Ltd. (see address under *Contemporary Serging,* above). Time: 60 minutes. Machines used: Hobbylock 794 and 795. $26.95 postpaid (transcript, $2.95). Rental, $6/week for Video Club members.

Sew 'n' Tell, ©1984, from the World of Sew Inc., Carriage Square, 1733 West 4160 South, Salt Lake City, UT 84119. Time: 101 minutes. Machines used: White Superlocks 503 and 534. $39.95 postpaid.

Sewing with Sergers—Advanced, ©
1989, Palmer/Pletsch Inc. (see address
under *Creative Serging,* above). Time:
60 minutes. Machines used: all
brands. $31.20 postpaid.

Sewing with Sergers —Basics, © 1989,
Palmer/Pletsch Inc. (see address under
Creative Serging, above). Time: 60
minutes. Machines used: all brands.
$31.20 postpaid.

Investigate the video market and
then take time for in-depth viewing
(while you serge?); you're sure to gain
valuable serger shortcuts and troubleshooting tips.

✎ **Note:** Staying current on serger
video titles is an ongoing task; titles are
discontinued and added on a frequent
basis. Video retailers like your local
dealer or mail-order companies like
Clotilde or Nancy's Notions (see pages
163-173 for addresses) can keep you
up-to-date. Nancy's Notions Video
Club has to be one of the most comprehensive video collections around. A
lifetime membership is $15, and as of
this publishing date, the club offered
over 110 titles. Also, watch for new
releases announced in the *Serger Update*
newsletter (see address below).

Sewing Publications

Butterick Home Catalog, 161 Sixth
Avenue, New York, NY 10013. $8 for
four issues annually.

McCall's Pattern Magazine, 230 Park
Avenue, New York, NY 10169. For a
four-issue annual subscription, $10.

Needle and Craft, 810 Seventh Ave.,
New York, NY 10019. A bimonthly
magazine—$15.97 a year. Don't miss
Robbie Fanning's "Commentary"
column on the last page of every issue.

Serger Update, 2269 Chestnut, Suite
269, San Francisco, CA 94123. The only
periodical devoted entirely to serging
news and techniques. Published
monthly ($36 annual subscription).

Sew It Seams, P.O. Box 2698, Kirkland,
WA 98083. $22 per year for this quar-
terly magazine.

Sew News, P.O. Box 1790, Peoria, IL
61656. $15.97 for an annual subscrip-
tion (12 monthly issues). Look for the
"Machines in Motion: Sergers" column,
written by Gail Brown and Sue Green.

Sewing Update (address is the same as
Serger Update). Newsletter format
without advertising (sister publication
to *Serger Update* newsletter). Sent every
other month—$18 per year. Also, see
the special sampler offer at the beginning of the book.

Vogue Patterns Magazine, 161 Sixth
Ave., New York, NY 10013. Subscrip-
tions are $12.95 annually, for six bi-
monthly issues.

About the Authors

Gail Brown is one of the most widely read writers in home sewing, and is recognized for her serger expertise, extensive research, and fast, innovative methods. She is Contributing Editor for the *Serger Update* newsletter and is the coauthor of three best-selling books on serger sewing, including *Creative Serging Illustrated*. Her work appears in *McCall's Pattern Magazine, Needle and Craft, Sewing Update, Sew News, The Singer Sewing Library* and *Vogue Patterns Magazine*. Although this home economics graduate started her career nearly 20 years ago in New York City, she now transmits via modem from the small coastal town of Hoquiam, Washington. Her patient husband, John Quigg, and two children, put up with her deadlines and growing collection of sergers, sewing machines, needlework collectibles, and computer paraphernalia.

Tammy Young has combined creativity and practicality in her writing and publishing career. Having worked for several years in the ready-to-wear fashion industry, she is known for her ability to translate retail trends into home-sewing techniques. Tammy is a graduate of Oregon State University and is a former extension agent and high school home economics teacher. Her recent titles include *Distinctive Serger Gifts and Crafts, An Idea Book for all Occasions*, and *Serged Gifts in Minutes!* Currently her office and home are located in downtown San Francisco, where she oversees all facets of *Update* newsletter and book production—editing, illustration direction, layout, and printing. When her hectic schedule allows, Tammy travels stateside and abroad, frequently picking up fashion and fabric trends for the *Update* newsletters and books.

Index

Alterations, instant, 105-107
    Adding slits, 106
    Letting out inseams, 106
Appliqués, 64-65
Authors, about the, 178
Ball-point serger needles, 143
Bead strands, 63
Bead trim, cross-locked glass, 41
Beading foot, 141
Belt loops, criss-crossed, 26
Bias binder foot, 141
Binding, elasticized, 29-30
Bite width, changing, 136-137
Blind-hem foot, 139
Blouse, tie, 96
Boiled wool, serging, 36-39
Books, serger 174
Buying a serger, considerations,
    147-149
    Cutting, 148
    Differential feed, 149
    Narrow rolled hems, 148
    Needles, 147
    Other options, 149
    Stitch capabilities, 147
    Lighting, 147
    Sewing Speed, 148
    Stitch length, 148
    Stitch width, 148
    Tension adjustability, 148
Circle Curtains, 128-129
Collar, wrapped and decoratively
    serged, 6-7
Collar, wrapped, 4-6
Collars, round, 2
Cord Cover-ups, 130
Corners, preventing too-pointed, 114
Couching (scrollwork), 57-60

Cover stitch, industrial, 14-15
Cover-up, quick serged, 92-93
Curtains
    Circle, 128-129
    Instant draped, 127-128
Cutting attachments for conventional
    machines, 151-152
Cutwork, serger, 65-67
Decor 6, 41
Decorative serging, 44-46
    How will it look, 46-47
    Steps to success, 44-46
Delicate fabrics, 1
Dress, one-piece, 95-96
Dressed-up Serging (special occasions),
    76-82
    Glitzy accents, 82
    Lamé, 80-81
    Sequins, 81-82
Edge finishing, 10-11
Elastic bands, exposed, 27
Elastic casing, two-step topstitched,
    28-29
Elastic guide foot, 139
Elastic, transparent (polyurethane), 10
Elastics, ready-to-wear applications,
    27-31
    Binding, elasticized, 29-30
Elastic casing, two-step topstitched,
    28-29
    Exposed elastic bands, 27
    Shirring, with elastic, 31
Embroidery floss (six-strand cotton), 41
Fabric jams, removing, 137-138
Facing applications, 3

Feet, for the serger, 139-141
    All-purpose foot, 139
    Beading foot, 141
    Blind-hem foot, 139
    Bias binder foot, 141
    Elastic guide foot, 139
    Piping foot, 140
    Snap-off foot, 139
    Tape guide foot, 141
Fishing line flounces, 60-62
Fit, fine-tuning, 103-105
    Flatlocking to lets seams out,
        105
    Lengthening hems, 105
    Preventive fitting, 103
    Serged basting, 104
    Taking in serged seams, 104
Five-thread sergers, buying considera
    tions, 150-151
Flatlocking
    Faux, 15
    Flatter, 49-50
    Floating, 51
Gathering, with serged chain, 11-13
Hems, serged and topstitched, 4
Holiday decorations, 131-133
    Garlands, 131
    Fabric ribbons, 132
    Layered tree skirt, 133
Hot serger hints, 142-144
    Cleaning without forced air, 143
    Easier threading, 142
    Jam-proofing, 143
    New needle options, 143
    Seam sealant in your machine,
        143
    Stitching accuracy, 142
Instant Draped Curtains, 127-128
Johnny collar, 17-18

Knit accessories, 88-92
    Rectangles, 90-91
    Triangles, 89-90
    Tubes, 92-92
Knits, modular, 18-21
Knitting, keyplate, 73-75
Melt adhesive thread (Thread-fuse™), 40
Menswear into women's wear, 110-111
Metallic threads, 42
Mock hemstitching, 14
Monofilament nylon, 41, 51-52
Napkin rings, 116
Napkins, 112-115
Needles, buying the right type and
    size, 152-153
Nylon thread, monofilament, 41
Pearl Crown Rayon, 41
Piping foot, 140
Piping, serged, 52-56
        Application, 55-56
        Bead trim piping, 55
        Twisted pearl cotton piping,
            53-54
Piping, stabilize with, 11
Placemats, mitered, 117-119
Plackets, seamed, 3
Pocket Squares, 87-88
Pockets, in-seam, 2
Polyurethane (transparent) elastic, 10
Planning, production-order
    Basic four-panel skirt, 97
    Basic one-piece dress, 95-96
    Basic thirty-minute slacks,
        98- 101
    Basic tie blouse, 96
Puckers, eliminating, 114
Rayon, pearl cotton, 41
Rethreading, so threads won't break,
    138
Reversible fashions and fabrics, 23-26
Ribbing, faux flatlocked, 16

Ribbing,
    Relaxed application, 72
    Serge-finished, 21-22
Ribbon Floss, 41
Ribbon Thread, 41
Scrollwork (couching), 57-60
Seams Great®, 52
Serge-by-Mail Directory, 163-174
    Cycling, hiking skiing, 170
    Dressmaker fabrics, 170-173
    Formals, proms, weddings, 168
    Lace, trims, ribbons, bead
      strands, sequins, 165
    Notions, 166-167
    Risk-free mail order, 163
    Sensational silks, 168
    Specialty patterns, 164
    Stretch knits, 169
Serged Ribbing Rose, 85-86
Sergeon, tips from, 144-145
Serger companies, 162
Serger Needle Guide (chart), 154-156
Sewing publications, 177
Sheet covers, 119-122
Shirring, with elastic, 31
Shoulder pads, contoured, 13
Skirt, four-panel, 97
Slacks, thirty-minute, 98-101
Sleeves, cuffs in, 3
Stitch glossary, 157-158
    Five-thread, 158
    Four/two thread, 157
    Three/four-thread mock safety
      stitch, 158
    Three/four-thread safety stitch,
      158
    Three-thread, 157
    Two-thread, 157
Stitch quality, improving, 134-137
    Changing bite width, 136-137
    Needle quality and position,
      134
    Position of blades, 134-135
    Thread quality, 135

Stitch terminology, 159-161
    Ease plus, 161
    Faux flatlocked, 160
    Balanced, 159
    Flatlocked, 159
    Narrow rolled edge or hem, 160
    Reversible edge binding, 160
    Taut serging, 161
Strip-patchwork and quilting, 122-127
    Exposed patchwork seams,
      125-126
    Reversible serger-strip quilting,
      126-127
Strip-pieced quilt, 122-124
Sweaterknits, 68-72
Sweaters, knit and serged, 73-75
Sweaters, recycling and altering,
    107-110
Tailoring—soft, serged, 35-36
Tailoring, serged, 32-34
Tape guide foot, 141
Thread-fuse™, melt adhesive thread, 40
Three/four-thread stitches,
    Flatlocking, 48-49
    Tuck-and-roll stitch, 47-48
Tinsel Twill, 42
Troubleshooting with Sue Green,
    137-139
    Removing fabric jams, 137-138
    Threads that keep breaking, 138
Tucks, tunnel, 2
Twist-to-Fit Sash, 83-85
Unraveling stitches, 102-103
Update Newsletter booklets, 175
Videos, serger, 176-177
Waistline, seams, 4
Woolly stretch nylon, 42
Wrapped tops, 22-23
Zippers, applications, 7-9

229.71
model # 71LG 38322N
219.88
38326
rear bag